I Forgive You

By

T. Dwayne Smith Sr.

I Forgive You
First Print Edition
ISBN 13: 978-0-9908109-2-6
Copyright © 2018, T. Dwayne Smith Sr., M.A., CLC

Unless otherwise indicated, all Scripture quotations are taken from the King James Version of the Bible.

Scripture quotations marked (AMP) taken from the Amplified® Bible Copyright © 1954, 1958, 1962, 1964, 1965, 1987 by The Lockman Foundation Used by permission.

Scripture quotations marked (NIV) are taken from the Holy Bible, New International Version®, NIV®. Copyright © 1973, 1978, 1984, 2011 by Biblica, Inc.™ Used by permission of Zondervan. All rights reserved worldwide. www.zondervan.com The "NIV" and "New International Version" are trademarks registered in the United States Patent and Trademark Office by Biblica, Inc.™

Scripture quotations marked (MSG) are taken from THE MESSAGE, copyright © 1993, 1994, 1995, 1996, 2000, 2001, 2002 by Eugene H. Peterson. Used by permission of NavPress. All rights reserved. Represented by Tyndale House Publishers, Inc.

Printed in the United States of America.
All rights reserved under International Copyright Law. Contents and / or cover may not be reproduced in whole or in part in any form without the express written consent of the author.

Team Unstoppable, Inc.

444 E Roosevelt, Rd. Suite #254, Lombard, IL 60148
708.218.1104

Teen-Train.org
tdwayne@teamunstoppable.org

Table of Contents

Book Reviews --------------------------------------- i
Acknowledgement ------------------------------- vii
Foreword -- xi
Introduction --- xv
  Chapter I: Beauty for Ashes ----------- 1
  Chapter II: Perfect Love -------------- 25
  Chapter III: Offense Will Come ---- 51
  Chapter IV: Faith to Forgive --------- 75
  Chapter V: The Key to Freedom --- 105
Salvation Prayer ---------------------------- 149
Forgiveness Confession ------------------ 153
Prayer for Backslide --------------------- 155

Book Reviews

What are people saying about <u>I Forgive You?</u>

T. Dwayne Smith is an insightful, powerful, thought provoking author, with words that are liberating and healing. He is a literary master who brings the thoughts and purposes of God's heart to his readers. T. Dwayne's writings have the power to propel generations out of the power of darkness into the marvelous light.

>Lisa Burnett
>City of Light Christian Arts Center
>www.cityoflightperformingartsandmentoring.org

I Forgive You is a book packed full of life lessons about forgiveness. This book also focuses on how having a clean heart, and right spirit are essential in order to give the gift of forgiveness to others just as Christ has, and continues to forgive us. These lessons were planted early in the life of author T. Dwayne Smith, when he had a face-to-face meeting with forgiveness after the loss of both parents.

> Dwight E. DeRamus, Jr.
> Educator/Certified Life Coach
> Author of Disappearing Dads
> www.disappearingdads.com

It is a blessing to be given the opportunity to express how fortunate I am to know author T. Dwayne Smith. Our friendship of nearly 20 years, is a brotherhood rooted in the love of God. Over the years, I have watched him pursue his dreams with admirable passion, and I have witnessed him overcome the kind of challenges that could not be done without the revelation of forgiveness. It is clear, God has imparted wisdom to T. Dwayne Smith in the area of forgiveness, that will provide a comprehensive understanding guaranteed to remove the heavy and painful burden of unforgiveness. I encourage you as you read this book to open your heart and allow the healing this anointed book will forge in your life to take place.

> Alvin Pickett, Jr.
> Entrepreneur

T. Dwayne Smith, has captured the essence and treasure of forgiveness for the individual, leading to liberty of the heart, mind, and soul. His ability to take the word of God, and apply it to the life of the hurting, betrayed, offended, battered, wounded, angered, and broken, for application and transformation of the person to a life of rejuvenation, joy, and peace is only released through intentional forgiveness. T. Dwayne's mission is to take the individual harboring unforgiveness to a place of understanding. T. Dwayne's ability to define unforgiveness and its effects on the person from internal to external corrosions of one's life, and its effects on relationships with others, are profound. Unforgiveness is a nasty root that extends and creates branches that become cancerous in nature. Unforgiveness is designed to kill hopes and steal dreams of having a healthy productive life. '*I Forgive You*,' is a gift you owe yourself as Dwayne exhibits in his book. If you are married, single, older or younger, *I Forgive You* is a treasure to be sought out and applied to all walks of life as forgiveness should be a lifestyle choice for every person on the face of the earth. Let this book take you from a place of bondage to a place of freedom through forgiveness.

Pastor Steven Ramos

When it comes to present day truth, passion, and relational wisdom T. Dwayne Smith remains relevant and consistent! *I Forgive You* is a very necessary tool and resource for the days and times for which we live. The bitter root of unforgiveness is one of the subtlest, yet equally dangerous and effective traps of the enemy to keep individuals and relationships stuck and limited. It is high time that the detrimental effects of deep hurt, pride, and unforgiveness be exposed and dealt with once and for all. Like peeling the layers of an onion, *I Forgive You* can uncover the most pungent catalysts of relational deprivation, and arrested development using the most practical methods! You need this book! Families need this book! Youth groups need this book! Churches need this book! EVERYONE needs this book! Invest in the generational freedom and peace that we all deserve. Healing is for the here and now - let it start with YOU.

>   Cicely Victoria
>   "The Firestarter"
>   Passion International

I want to first of all congratulate my friend and brother in Christ, T. Dwayne Smith on this awesome labor of love. His sense of timing is truly commendable, because our world has entered a very harsh season of division, hurt, strife and unforgiveness. I believe that everyone who reads this book will gain a better perspective about this issue of forgiveness and how to live and walk in it. Each one of us has experienced the trauma of being hurt, neglected, or abused by others which has led to periods of extended anger and frustration. The initial anger and hurt we experience when unfortunate disappointments occur, are well understood by God. God says to "be angry but do not sin." There are two main sins that we commit when we are offended, retaliation and unforgiveness. This book will help you discover the reason why we must make this life-liberating decision to forgive. T. Dwayne Smith's testimonies are sincere and will in fact help millions of people who have lost themselves in unforgiveness. I am truly honored to have this opportunity to share this brief perspective on how important this book is for all of us who will heed its wisdom. All of us who will open our hearts to receive the message. God bless you!

> Reverend Terrence E. Trimuel, Sr.
> Author of Divorce Your Debt: A Spiritual Journey From Self Debt to Deliverance

I have no doubt this book will be a blessing to everyone who reads it. To forgive, despite the offense -- to love past the hurt--to have faith, when there is no obvious reason to forgive, is the key to freedom. T. Dwayne has been blessed to be a blessing to the world. Allow what God has given him to be a blessing to you today!

> Stephanie Johnson
> Educator
> Proud Mom of a Teen-Train. Inc., Alum

Acknowledgement

To my Lord and Savior, Jesus Christ: Thank You for Your Life and Your example of Humanity, Grace, Love and Forgiveness. You are the ultimate example of LOVE! Thank you for forgiving us and teaching us how to Forgive others. Thank Jesus for the example You set before us. You are the ultimate example of love! Thank You for forgiving us and teaching us how to forgive others.

To my beautiful wife: Tannita, thank you for being my best friend, always supporting me, and standing by my side! Daily, you teach me through your love for me what forgiveness is about in marriage. You are an amazing woman and I thank God for you. I'm forever grateful to have you as my wife. I love you!

To my Siblings; John, Delores and Jeanine: Thank you for your love, support, prayers, and encouragement. When I was going through my darkest and most challenging moments in life, you were there to support me and to encourage me. I appreciate you and love you dearly. I appreciate our time growing up together and I love you all dearly!

To my children; Josh, Jeremiah, TJ, Timothy, and Jon: God has a plan for your lives. Don't allow unresolved hurt and disappointment to hinder or stop God's will from coming to pass in your lives! Trust in the Lord with all your hearts and lean not to your own understanding. Acknowledge God in all your ways, and He will direct your paths. Love you all dearly!

To the millions of people who have been hurt, disappointed, taken for granted, misused, betrayed and abused. Today, I challenge you to make a decision to forgive! Forgiveness is a very difficult process. The first step to make along this journey is the decision to forgive. In my opinion, the most liberating and empowering words you can speak are the words, I forgive you! These words will free you from the bondage of your past and give you a brand new start on life. In my opinion, the three most liberating and empowering words that transcend race, gender, age, ethnicity, and religion are the words, "**I forgive you!**" Don't let unforgiveness blindside you and keep you traveling on the road of self-destruction. When you forgive, you break the power of past hurts and disappointments in your life. When you forgive, you allow God to fight battles on your behalf. When you forgive, you are finally free!

> *"Beloved never avenge yourselves, but leave the way open for God's wrath {and His judicial righteousness}; for it is written {in Scripture}, "Vengeance is Mine, I will repay," says the Lord."*
>
> - Romans 12:19 AMP

Make the decision to forgive so that you can embrace true freedom and fulfill your destiny today!

God Bless You!
T. Dwayne Smith Sr.

Special Acknowledgement

To My Lovely Wife, Tannita A. Smith;

You came along when I was down. Through thick and thin you have been around. You have been my rock, my motivation, my greatest supporter. Every time I wanted to give up, you would not allow me to quit. Every time I wanted to complain, you helped me to refocus. Every time I wanted to say enough is enough, you challenged me to go another step further. When I look at the challenges, obstacles, and barriers that you have had to overcome in your own personal life, I see a woman of grace, compassion, and strength. Tannita, your life has been a true testament of God's word in action. When I look at you, I see the manifestation of Proverbs 31:10-30.

> *"An excellent woman (one who is spiritual, capable, intelligent, and virtuous), who is he who can find her? Her value is more precious than jewels and her worth is far above rubies or*

pearls. The heart of her husband trust in her (with secure confidence), And he will have no lack of gain. She comforts, encourages, and does him only good and not evil all the days of her life. She looks for wool and flax and works with willing hands in delight. She rises also while it is still night and gives food to her household and assigns tasks to her maids. She considers a field before she buys or accepts it (expanding her business prudently); With her profits she plants fruitful vines in her vineyard. She equips herself with strength (spiritual, mental, and physical fitness for her God-given task) and makes her arms strong. She sees that her gain is good; Her lamp does not go out, but it burns continually through the night (she is prepared for whatever lies ahead). She stretches out her hands to the distaff, and her hands hold the spindle (as she spins wool into thread for clothing). She opens and extends her hand to the poor, and she reaches out her filled hands to the needy. She does not fear the snow for her household, for all in her household are clothed in (expensive) scarlet (wool). She makes for herself coverlets, cushions, and rugs of tapestry. Her clothing is linen, pure and fine, and purple (wool). Her husband "Dwayne" is known in the (city's) gates, when he sits among the elders of the land. She makes (fine) linen garments and sells them; and supplies sashes to the merchants. Strength and dignity are her clothing and her position is strong and secure; and she smiles at the future (knowing that she and her family are prepared). She opens her mouth in (skillful and godly) wisdom, and the teaching of kindness is on her tongue (giving counsel and instruction). She looks well to how things go in her household, and does not eat the bread of idleness. Her children rise up and call her blessed (happy, prosperous, to be admired); Her husband also, and he praises her, saying, "Many daughters have done nobly, and well (with the strength of character that is steadfast in goodness), But you "Tannita Smith" excel them all." Charm and grace are deceptive, and (superficial) beauty is vain, but a woman who fears the Lord (reverently worshiping, obeying, serving, and trusting Him will awe-filled respect), she shall be praised."

Tannita, you totally embody Proverbs 31:10-30 in word, deed, and faith. I love you and I trust you with my heart. I feel secure and safe with you! Your faith, love, and confidence in the Lord Jesus Christ has allowed you to walk in forgiveness and to teach forgiveness to others through faith in God's word. Watching you practice forgiveness reminds me of God's love and mercy that is extended to us daily. Tannita, you are the love of my life and I thank God that He not only restored my life, He gave me the wife of my dreams!
I LOVE YOU!

FORWARD

It is said that agitation leads to change, but change is not change at all without growth. While things are changing all around us every day—growth still remains an option. It is up to the individual to adapt to the change, and consequently grow. When situations, circumstances, and relationships of our lives agitate us, and cause us to become uncomfortable—it is then our responsibility to make the decision to change.

One of the greatest opportunities for growth that is spawned by change, is the ability to forgive, release, and let go. Let go of past failures, let go of disappointments, let go of broken relationships, dashed hopes, and unmet expectations in those we have put our deepest trust in.

Throughout my time of knowing T. Dwayne Smith Sr., I have seen him grow in leaps and bounds. It takes one to know his story and appreciate how he has grown through the winds of change in his life. I believe as you read through the pages of this book, you will begin to see that T. Dwayne Smith epitomizes, what it means to grow through the change of forgiveness.

As you read through this book you'll discover that forgiveness is more a decision, than it is an experience or emotional feeling of release. Each day we decide to forgive, is a day that we have decided to enhance the quality of our lives, and free ourselves to be the person God ordained us to become.

Through every hardship, let down, disappointment, attack, and seeming setback, my friend and brother, T. Dwayne Smith has endured and weathered faithfully. He has shown a tremendous resolve to love and to forgive!

The late Booker T. Washington is quoted as saying, "he will never allow a man to belittle his soul by making him hate another human being." Make the decision today to forgive and be free!

Osazee O. Thompson,
Author, Empowerment Conference Speaker, and Certified Life Coach
www.OsazeeThompson.com

Introduction

Forgiveness is defined by *American Dictionary of The English Language (Webster's 1828)* as: **To pardon; to remit, as an offense or debt; to overlook an offense, and treat the offender as not guilty.**

What's in Your Heart?
- Have you ever been mistreated?
- Have you ever been lied on?
- Have you ever been betrayed?
- Have you ever been hurt by someone you loved?
- Have you ever been abused or misused?

If you answered "yes" to any of these questions, you are one of millions who has had to deal with hurt inflicted by the words or actions of another. Hurt can take many forms: unwarranted criticism, a project sabotaged at the hands of a classmate or colleague, broken promises, or infidelity. The emotional wounds can leave you with lasting feelings of hurt; rejection, emptiness, brokenness, confusion, anger, bitterness, and a desire for revenge.

The feelings from the experience don't always go away with time. As a matter-of-fact, the pain can grow deeper and deeper within your heart over time. Your mind has the potential and capacity to relive the experience like a scratched record playing the same chorus. You purposely block out the past hurts, but certain triggers can take you right back to that very moment. Vividly, you remember what you were wearing, what you were eating, the time of day, the season of the year, the smell in the air, and the emotions you felt as a result of the traumatic experience. You may wonder why the feelings still grip you today, even though the experience took place some five, ten, or even twenty years ago? The reason why it's so hard to shake off the hurt and move past the experience is because we sometimes think that forgetting is forgiving and that is often interpreted as a sign of weakness. We sometimes feel that we need to hold on to the hurt as a form of education to guide our thoughts and our actions. In other cases, we feel the need to hold on to the memories of our past hurts in order to establish and maintain boundaries when dealing with other people. Most times, we just think the offender doesn't deserve to be forgiven. So, we justify our position and provide a safe harbor for our unforgiving thoughts because it gives us some sense of control and power. It's hard to release the feelings of hurt, rejection, offense, anger, and bitterness because these feelings are now entrenched in our heart. Whatever your situation may be, moving past any hurt is never an easy task.

I once heard someone say that the heaviest weight a person can carry is a GRUDGE! A grudge is defined by the Merriam-Webster Dictionary as:
1. A feeling of deep-seated resentment or ill will towards another person;
2. Harbored feeling of resentment that seeks satisfaction;
3. To dislike or feel angry towards someone or something;
4. A strong feeling or angry towards someone that lasts for a long time.

When someone you love and trust hurts you, there is a tendency to become angry, upset, and offended. If you dwell in this place of hurt, without addressing the root cause of the emotional pain, deep-seated resentment, dislike, vengeance, and hostility develops in your heart towards the individual that hurt you.

The interesting thing about offenses is that offenses are like trees--they have roots. When you look at a tree, you see the leaves or the fruit, but you never see the roots. The unseen roots are the life source of the tree. I was once told that the height of a tree is an indicator of the depth of its roots. Like a tree, when you outwardly display strong dislike and resentment, it's an indicator of the depth of hurt that has grown and continues to grow deep inside your heart.

What Goes In, Must Come Out!

Forgiveness is never about the other person, it is always about you! It's about peace in your mind. It's about peace in your heart. It's about peace in your life, and most importantly, it's about peace in your relationship with God. You deserve PEACE!

When faced with the challenges of past and present offenses, lies, and betrayal, it can be extremely difficult to overcome these challenges. However, like the author of self-awareness books, *Lover of Life*, and *"Philosopher of Happiness,"* Jonathan Lockwood Huie said, "it's not about the other person deserving the forgiveness, it's about you deserving peace."

People have a tendency to cling to unforgiveness as a sense of control and power without understanding the cost. What goes in, must come at some point and time in your life. The negative feelings that you harbor inside your heart towards another person will begin to crowd out positive feelings, and eventually you will be overcome by your own bitterness and unforgiveness. If you refuse to deal with the unforgiveness in your heart, it can lead to more complex life issues such as bringing unresolved anger and bitterness into new relationships and unwanted sickness in your body. These negative experiences are designed to consume you with the wrongs of your past and hinder your ability to enjoy the possibilities of a new and brighter future. If you do not guard your heart from unforgiveness, you will begin to experience a deep sense of lost purpose and meaning, while developing a mindset of doubt, skepticism, anxiety, and apprehensiveness. If this vicious cycle continues, it will lead to broken relationships, feelings of loneliness, trust issues, sense of hopelessness, uncontrolled emotions, a negative outlook on new opportunities, and a host of other mental health issues.

"Forgive others not because they deserve forgiveness but because you deserve peace."
 - Jonathan Lockwood Huie, Author of self-awareness books, Lover of Life, and "Philosopher of Happiness"

Forgiveness is a Decision, Not a Feeling!

Joyce Meyer, Charismatic Christian author, speaker and president of Joyce Meyer Ministries, described forgiveness as a decision not a feeling. Joyce goes on to say, "forgiveness is not a feeling – it's a decision we make because we want to do what is right before God. It's a quality decision that won't be easy and it may take time to get through the process, depending on the severity of the offense."

When you make the decision to forgive, the offender is not released from their wrong doing. You release yourself from the grip of the grudge. You sever the root of resentment from feeding and growing in your heart. When you forgive, it doesn't mean that the offenses did not occur. It means that you have made a conscious decision to deny your past access into your future. When you decide to forgive; you open your heart to God so He can manifest the promise He made in Ezekiel 11:19-20 (AMP):

> **"And I will give them one heart (a new heart), and put a new spirit within them. I take from them the heart of stone, and will give them a heart of flesh (that is responsive to My touch), that they may walk in My statutes and keep My ordinances and do them."**

A heart that is responsive to the touch of God is a heart that is void of bitterness and unforgiveness. God wants to heal you and give you a heart of compassion and love toward anyone who has hurt you.

When you forgive, you are not in any way denying the other person's responsibility for the hurt in your life. Your decision to forgive has nothing to do with the other person deserving forgiveness. Your decision to forgive gives you peace and freedom to move forward in your life. When you forgive, you give yourself access to the following benefits: personal happiness, good health, peace of mind, spiritual freedom, healthy relationships, self-efficacy, joy, wealth, blessings, and an optimistic outlook on life.

What's in Your Heart?

Regardless of the Bible version you read—be it Amplified, Message, King James or New International—the Bible warns us to guard what goes into our heart in Proverbs 4:23.

> **"Watch over your heart with all diligence, for from it flows the springs of life." (Amp)**
>
> **"Keep vigilant watch over your heart; that's where life starts". (MSG)**
>
> **"Above all else, guard your heart, for everything you do flows from it." (NIV)**

The Bible further expounds on the topic of the matters of the heart in Mark 7:20,

> **"Whatever comes from (the heart of) a man, that is what defiles and dishonors him. For from within, (that is) out the heart of men, come base and malevolent thoughts and schemes, acts of sexual immorality, thefts, murders, adulteries, acts of greed and covetousness, wickedness, deceit, unrestrained**

conduct, envy and jealousy, slander and profanity, arrogance and self-righteousness and foolishness (poor judgment). All these evil things (schemes and desires) come from within and defile and dishonor the man".

Hebrews 12:15 (AMP),
"See to it that no one falls short of God's grace: that no root of resentment springs up and causes trouble, and by it many be defiled…"

The Bible says in Luke 6:45 (NIV),
"A good man brings good things out of the good stored up in his heart, and an evil man brings evil things out of the evil stored up in his heart. For the mouth speaks what the heart is full of."

The word of God is very clear about the matters of the heart and how the issues of the heart can set the course of your future--either good or bad. You can't control the choices that others make but you can control how you respond.

When you choose not to forgive, you say "Yes" to your past and "No" to your future. When you choose not to forgive, you forfeit new relationships and new experiences. When you choose not to forgive, you open yourself to sickness and disease. When you choose not to forgive, you remain enslaved to the person who hurt you.

However, when you choose to forgive, you say "Yes" to God and His will for your life! When you choose to forgive, you allow God to remove the hurt through His love and mend any brokenness in your life. When you choose to forgive, you take your power back. This doesn't mean the thoughts of past hurts will not come again. It means that you are now allowing God to replace the pain in your life with His love and His promises to deliver you. Now, the healing process, step-by-step, day-by-day can begin to take its course in your life.

When you forgive you won't change your past, but you sure do change your future. My prayer is that as you read this book, you will come to understand God's unfathomable love for you and His delivering power that is available for your life. God has a wonderful plan for your life. You were born with purpose, value, and great potential! Don't allow unforgiveness to kill, steal, and destroy your future. So, again I ask you—**what's in your heart?**

Chapter I
Beauty For Ashes!

"And provide for those who grieve in Zion- to bestow on them a crown of beauty instead of ashes, the oil of joy instead of mourning, and a garment of praise instead of a spirit of despair. They will be called oaks of righteousness, a planting of the Lord for the display of his splendor."

- Isaiah 61:3 (NIV)

"When you forgive, you in no way change the past – but you sure do change the future."
-Bernard Meltzer, United States radio host.

I remember growing up as a kid on the westside of Chicago feeling rejected, alone, broken, confused, and full of anger after the death of my mother. As a young boy, I did not understand what was going on with my mother's health and why she was so

I Forgive You

frequently in and out of the hospital. My mother was full of life, joy, and love. She was committed to God and her family. My mother always had a smile on her face and she consistently encouraged us as children to develop our relationship with God through a daily life of prayer and reading the Bible. Every night--without fail--my mother had the entire family praying the

Lord's Prayer in Luke 11:2-4;

> *"Our Father which art in heaven, Hallowed be thy name. Thy kingdom come. They will be done on earth as it is in heaven. Give us this day by day our daily bread. And forgive us our sins; for we also forgive everyone that is indebted to us. And lead us not into temptation; but deliver us from evil."*

What I did not realize then, but I now understand that my mother was teaching us through citing this prayer how to develop trust and faith in God, while at the same time, seeking God's forgiveness and extending forgiveness to others. Later on in life, I would learn to appreciate this very powerful biblical principle taught to me as a kid.

During the time my mother was dealing with her medical challenges, I remember her always saying to us, "don't worry about me," "everything was going to be okay," "have faith in God" and "don't forget to pray every night before going to sleep." In honor of our mother's request my older brother and sister would make sure that we continued our tradition of nightly prayer before going to sleep.

Over time, I became increasingly frustrated and angry with my mother because I didn't understand what was going on with her. Nobody, including my father took the time to explain my mother's medical condition. We did not understand how to support her, let alone how to navigate without her being around. I remember a time my mother was home, but she was physically weak and bedridden. I was so excited to have her home. I was looking forward to staying home from school and spending the day with her. However, like a responsible parent, my mother required me and my younger sister to go to school because she valued education and did not want us to miss any days out of school. However, my mother allowed my older brother and sister to stay home because she needed their support with cooking, cleaning, and other household chores. My younger sister and I were angry and upset. We thought her decision was so unfair. Jeanine and I were the youngest of four children and we were not afforded the same opportunities to visit our mother while she was in the hospital. Needless to say, we really looked forward to the opportunities of spending time with her when she came home from the hospital. I didn't know at the time that my mother was battling

I Forgive You

tuberculosis and diabetes. Some days would be better than others, and as my mother's condition worsened the pressure began to build and negatively impact our household.

Today's medical research, treatment, prevention, and nutritional knowledge was not available at that time. The lack of information and resources further exacerbated my mother's condition. My mother eventually became completely bedridden, and later on hospitalized for an extended time. She would occasionally come home for short home visits—no more than four or five hours at a time then, return to the hospital to avoid further medical complications. This put a lot of stress and pressure on my father as the primary care provider for four children and working a full-time job. My mother's absence from the home allowed us to see and value her contribution and worth. She was the glue that kept the home intact. Everything we needed, my mother made sure we had as a family including spiritual growth and development. My siblings and I felt alone and lost without the structure our mother provided when she was absent from home. I remember, one day I was in my mother's bedroom watching television. My curiosity got the better of me and I began looking through the colorful pages of her Bible. I came across a letter my mother wrote to God that changed my outlook on life that very moment. This was no ordinary letter I soon discovered. My mother was asking God to take her life so all the suffering she was dealing with in her body would finally be over. My eyes began to swell with tears as I continued to read those painful words, "Lord take my life now and take care of my husband and children." I was really confused. Why would my mother ask a loving God to take her life? My mother did not say in this letter Lord, heal my body! Nor did she did ask God to give her quality time with her children. My mother asked God to take her life so she would not have to suffer any longer. My heart became so overwhelmed with emotions. I couldn't take anymore, so I closed the Bible and began to cry. I was so deeply hurt by my mother's words. I became enraged all at once. I couldn't believe my mother was asking God to take her away and leave us behind. This didn't make any sense to me. I wanted to say something to my mother, but I remember that I had no business looking through her personal items in the first place so I kept it secret and carried the pain in my heart. When I looked at my mother, I felt hurt. I carried these feelings inside, and instead of enjoying the precious moments when my mother was home, I distanced myself and remained sulky and quiet. The anger, resentment, and disappointment towards my mother grew day-by-day. An internal battle waged on in my heart and I was losing day-by-day.

The day my mother made her transition, I remember having this horrible dream that seemed so real. Literally, I could feel the tears streaming down my face as I slept or so I thought. Suddenly, I hear two

I Forgive You

voices calling my name, "Dwayne, wake up!" My grandmother and aunt informed me and my brother John that our mother passed away in the hospital last night. I was devastated! This was a very stressful and painful time in my life because all I could remember seeing was my mother's written prayer request asking God to take her life! I felt cheated by God and my mother! I was hurt, confused, angry, and bitter with my mother and God. Losing my mother really took a toll on me. I fell into a state of depression, hopelessness, and continuous contemplation about the value and purpose of my life.

After the death of my mother, my father tried to bring some sense of normalcy back to the family through attending church and family functions. I was trying my best to make the adjustment to life without my mother. I was really missing her but I was also very angry with her for dying and leaving me and my siblings behind. My family didn't know what was going on with me because I was very quiet. I began to internalize my feelings. The negative thoughts and feelings were starting to manifest in other areas of my life. I developed a strong disinterest for learning, I started acting out in school, and I started to get into fights. I experienced deep sadness and anger around birthdays, holidays, and especially Mother's Day. My outlook on life became negative and pessimistic. I started to develop trust issues, and insecurities within my relationships. I didn't realize it then, but bitterness had taken root in my heart and it began to negatively impact my life and everything around me. The scripture says in Hebrews 12:15 (MSG):

> *"Make sure no one gets left out of God's generosity. Keep a sharp eye out for weeds of bitter discontent. A thistle or two gone to seed can ruin a whole garden in no time."*

Several years later, my father passed away from a massive heart attack before my very eyes. Prior to my father's death, our relationship was strained. There were a number of reasons, but the primary reason was my negative outlook on life. The feelings of hurt I experienced after the death of my father continued to feed the weed of discontentment that was growing at a rapid rate in my heart. The seed grew daily because of a lack of knowledge and understanding and it was watered daily with my negative thoughts and words. The seed was now bearing fruit in my life evidenced in my attitude, speech, and actions. The weeds of bitter discontent in my heart were defiling me and everything around me. I lost my joy, my spark for life, my desire to dream and my will to press through tough times. I remember moments in my life where all I did was harbor the negative thoughts of hurt, disappointment, and loneliness. I didn't want friends or family around me. I wanted to be alone all the time. I didn't realize it at that time, but I had developed a condition known as attachment disorder due to the failure to form normal attachments with my parents. I was also

struggling with a condition known as adjustment disorder as a result of the emotional trauma of dealing with the loss of my parents. It was difficult coping and dealing with these stressful life events that changed my outlook on life. I was driven by the fear of loss and it became my defense mechanism for managing my relationships and my emotions. I feared that if I allowed anyone else to get too close to me, they would eventually disappointment me and leave me brokenhearted.
Never Again!

What Goes In, Must Come Out!

What goes in your heart will eventually come out at some point in your life. The negative feelings that I was carrying inside my heart began to crowd out positive feelings and eventually, I was totally overcome by bitterness and unforgiveness. At that time in my life, I didn't understand what emotions I was dealing with so I decided not to deal with anything. I soon learned, as I got older and experienced more in life, that unresolved unforgiveness in your heart lead to more complex life issues. More negative experiences -major and minor- continued to feed the feelings and thoughts of people hurting me more and more. These thoughts impacted my life to the point that I became numb and rejected new possibilities and experiences. What I didn't know at that time, was that unforgiveness had taken root in my heart. I found myself with a loss sense of purpose and personal value. These feelings were compounded with depression, doubt, skepticism, anxiety, apprehensiveness, and a negative outlook on new opportunities. This vicious cycle continued in my life which lead to more broken relationships, feelings of loneliness, trust issues, and a strong sense of hopelessness. What was in my heart was definitely coming out in more ways than one.

Putting the Axe to The Root!

The root of bitterness was in my heart and it was producing bad fruit in my life. Thank God for His word in Luke 3:9 (NIV)

> *"The ax is already at the root of the trees, and every tree that does not produce good fruit will be cut down and thrown into the fire."*

God is so faithful that even when we are faithless and stuck in sin, He is a God of love and integrity and He will (actively) watch over His word to fulfill it.

The Bible tells us some of the following things about the nature and character of God:

God's Love (John 3:16),
God's Integrity (Numbers 23:19),
God's Faithfulness (1Corinthians 1:9),
God's Compassion (Psalms 111:4),

I Forgive You

God's Forgiveness (1John 1:9),
God's Mercy (Luke 1:78),
God's plan for Mankind (Genesis 1:28).

"To forgive is to set a prisoner free and discover that the prisoner was you."
- Lewis B. Smedes, <u>renowned Christian author, ethicist, and theologian in the Reformed tradition.</u>

God began to send people into my life with His word to be that "ax" for the cutting, pruning, and removal process of every tree that was not producing good fruit in my life. These individuals along with my sisters and brother helped me to see that God hadn't forgotten about me and He was actively watching over His word to fulfill it in my life. These individuals would minister to me, challenge my negative thinking, and repeatedly invite me to attend church. I eventually made Jesus the Lord of my life, and God brought to pass the promise He made to me in Ezekiel 36:26

> *"Moreover, I will give you a new heart and put a new spirit within you, and I will remove the heart of stone from your flesh and give you a heart of flesh."*

God removed the weight of despair and hopelessness. He forgave me and reminded me of the Lord's prayer that my mother taught us and had us pray nightly before bed. The Lord showed me that even though my parents were deceased, I could forgive them and release them from any hurt or disappointments in my heart. God delivered me from bitterness, unforgiveness, past hurts, emotional pain, and disappointments in my life. God reminded me that He will never leave me nor will He forsake me. God gave me a new heart of compassion, love, and forgiveness! God assured me that He approved of me and I didn't need anybody else's approval!

> *"Before I formed you in the womb I knew you (and <u>approved of you</u> as My chosen instrument), And before you were born I consecrated you (to Myself as My own); I have appointed you as a prophet to the nations."*
>
> - Jeremiah 1:5 (AMP)

God said to me that He knew me, approved me, chose me, consecrated me, and appointed me for greatness before I was formed in my mother's womb and before I experienced any trauma in my life. God had me all the while, and His plan for my life was already established before any trouble showed up in my life. The promise was here before the problem. Now, all I had to do was focus on the promise then, I would see that the problem was only a distraction. Problems are meant to distract you from the Promise!

<u>Problems are meant to distract you from the Promise!</u>

I Forgive You

Before the death of my parents, I remember God showing me visions of me helping other people. I would see myself in a leadership role advising, coaching, counseling, mentoring, teaching, lecturing, and motivating youth to pursue purpose and destiny in their lives. All of a sudden, people started to call me preacher and counselor. I didn't think twice about it as a kid, but I realize like Joseph's life in the Bible, God was showing me a forecast of my future. I often think about the story of Joseph who endured a lot of emotional trauma, disappointment, and setbacks yet he kept his heart right towards God and the people who mistreated him. As a young boy, God gave Joseph dreams of him leading and ruling over nations and God remained faithful to watch (actively) over His word until it came to pass in Joseph's life.

> *"Joseph had a dream, and when he told it to his brothers, and they hated him all the more. He said to them, "Listen to this dream I had: We were binding sheaves of grain out in the field when suddenly my sheaf rose and stood upright, while your sheaves gathered around mine and bowed down to it." His brothers said to him, "Do you intend to reign over us? Will you actually rule us? And they hated him all the more because of his dream and what he had said. Then he had another dream, and he told it to his brothers. "Listen," he said, "I had another dream, and this time the sun and moon and eleven stars were bowing down to me." When he*

> *told his father as well as his brothers, his father rebuked him and said, "What is this dream you had? Will your mother and I and your brothers actually come and bow down to the ground before you?" His brothers were jealous of him, but his father kept the matter in mind."*
> - Genesis 37:3-11 (NIV)

God gave Joseph a vision of leadership and influence as a young boy. Joseph didn't fully understand the vision. I believe Joseph innocently shared the vision with his family hoping they would embrace what God was showing him. Contrary, to what Joseph thought, his brothers despised him and his father rebuked him. I'm sure Joseph was devastated behind their reactions. After all, the last people you expect to reject you, talk about you, hate you, and display jealous over your success is your family! As a result of the hatred and jealously that was in the heart of Joseph's brothers, they teased him, bullied him, and contemplated killing him. One of the brothers convinced the others to spare Joseph's life, sell him into slavery, and lie to their father that Joseph was devoured by some ferocious animal. (Gen. 37:13-36)

When Joseph was taken to Egypt, the Bible says "the Lord was with Joseph" and even though he was enslaved, he became successful and prosperous. Potiphar was Joseph's master and he was able to see that God's hand was on Joseph. The Bible says the Lord caused all that Joseph did to prosper or succeed.

I Forgive You

As a result of witnessing the power of God on Joseph's life, Joseph found favor in the eyes of Potiphar. Potiphar made Joseph overseer in his house and placed him in charge over all that he owned. Everything was good for Joseph. Then, all of a sudden, Potiphar's wife started to make sexual advances towards Joseph. Joseph resisted the sexual temptation. However, Potiphar's wife falsely accused him of sexual assault. As a result of her claims, Joseph was put into prison for a crime he did not commit. The Bible says again that the Lord was with Joseph and gave him favor in the sight of the warden (Gen. 39:1-23). If we fast forward to Genesis chapter 50, Joseph is totally exonerated and restored back into power. God positioned Joseph to manage the financial affairs of Egypt. The dream God gave Joseph came to pass just as God promised. Joseph was in a position of leadership and influence in Egypt and everyone moved to his commands. After the death of their father, Joseph's brothers grew concerned. They felt Joseph would seek revenge for how they mistreated him.

> *"When Joseph's brothers saw that their father was dead, they said, "What if Joseph carries a grudge against us and pay us back in full for all the wrong which we did to him?' So they sent word to Joseph, saying, "Youth father commanded us before he died, saying, "You are to say to Joseph, "I beg you, please forgive the transgression of your brothers and their sin, for*

Beauty For Ashes

they did you wrong." Now, please forgive the transgression of the servants of the God of your father." And Joseph wept when they spoke to him. Then his brothers went and fell down before him (in confession); then they said, Behold, we are your servants (slaves)." But Joseph said to them, "Do not be afraid, for am I in the place of God? (Vengeance is His, not mine.) As for you, you meant evil against me, but God meant it for good in order to bring about this present outcome, that many people would be kept alive (as they are this day). So now, do not be afraid; I will provide for you and support you and your little ones." So he comforted them (giving them encouragement and hope) and spoke (with kindness) to their hearts."

- Gen. 50:14-22 (AMP)

Joseph like myself and so many others had plenty of time and opportunity to reflect, meditate, and relive negative experiences suffered over the years. It doesn't matter how big or small the incident, hurt is hurt! In my case, I was suffering from childhood pain and disappointments unbeknownst to my parents. In Joseph's case, his brothers willingly mistreated him without any consideration for those that were hurt in the process. Knowingly or unknowingly, emotional scares and grudges form over time if not properly addressed.

I Forgive You

"It's one of the greatest gifts you can give yourself, to forgive. Forgive everybody."
-Maya Angelou, an American poet, singer, memoirist, and civil rights activist.

God showed me that He loved me and He forgave me. So, it was my responsibility as a Christian (follower of Christ) to forgive my parents, myself, and everyone else who hurt me. Joseph forgave his brothers. When Joseph's brothers came and threw themselves down before him and pleaded for mercy and forgiveness, Joseph responded, "Do not be afraid, for am I in the place of God? (Vengeance is His, not mine.) Gen. 50:19 (AMP). I believe Joseph understood God's word in Matthew 6:15

> ***But if you do not forgive others their sins, your Father will not forgive your sins."***

Joseph knew that his help came from the Lord and he put his hope and trust in God. God not only delivered Joseph, God turned everything that was meant for evil for Joseph's good.

Beauty for Ashes…
> ***"And provide for those who grieve in Zion- to bestow on them a crown of beauty instead of ashes, the oil of joy instead of mourning, and a garment of praise instead of a spirit of despair. They will be called oaks of righteousness, a***

Chapter I: Beauty for Ashes!

Key Principles
- God gives you beauty for ashes.
- What the enemy meant for evil, God will turn for your good!
- You must forgive in order to be forgiven!
- The promise was here before the problem!
- Forgiveness is personal!
- Forgiveness is the key to unlocking your future.
- God wants you to be successful!

Meditation Scriptures:

Isaiah 61:3
"And provide for those who grieve in Zion- to bestow on them a crown of beauty instead of ashes, the oil of joy instead of mourning, and a garment of praise instead of a spirit of despair. They will be called oaks of righteousness, a planting of the Lord for the display of his splendor."

Luke 11:2-4
"Our Father which art in heaven, Hallowed be thy name. Thy kingdom come. They will be done on earth as it is in heaven. Give us this day by day our daily bread. And forgive us our sins; for we also forgive everyone that is indebted to us. And lead us not into temptation; but deliver us from evil."

I Forgive You

Hebrews 12:15
"Make sure no one gets left out of God's generosity. Keep a sharp eye out for weeds of bitter discontent. A thistle or two gone to seed can ruin a whole garden in no time."

Luke 3:9
"The ax is already at the root of the trees, and every tree that does not produce good fruit will be cut down and thrown into the fire."

Ezekiel 36:26
"Moreover, I will give you a new heart and put a new spirit within you, and I will remove the heart of stone from your flesh and give you a heart of flesh."

Jeremiah 1:5
"Before I formed you in the womb I knew you (and <u>approved of you</u> as My chosen instrument), And before you were born I consecrated you (to Myself as My own); I have appointed you as a prophet to the nations."

Mark 11:24-26
"Therefore, I tell you, whatever you ask for in prayer, believe that you received it, and it will be yours. And when you stand praying, if you hold anything against anyone, forgive them so that your Father in heaven may forgive you your sins."

Chapter I: Reflection Questions

What does beauty for ashes mean to you in the context of forgiving?

_____
_____
_____
_____
_____
_____
_____

Reflect on a personal situation in your life when you were challenged with unforgiveness. Describe the nature of the hurt and share why forgiving was a challenge for you.

_____
_____
_____
_____
_____
_____
_____
_____
_____

I Forgive You

What is your initial reaction to the concept of forgiving? Do you react in denial, anger, emotional outbursts, lashing out, or retaliation? Do you feel that your resolution for dealing with unforgiveness brings lasting peace, or leads to more pain and frustration?

_____
_____
_____
_____
_____
_____
_____
_____

As you reflect on the chapter, and some of the personal information that the author shared about his life experiences, ask yourself the following questions:

- **What?**
- **So, what?**
- **Now, what?**

Begin with defining and sharing **"what"** facts and events the author shared in the chapter, *Beauty For Ashes*.

"So, what" did you learn about yourself as a result of what the author shared?

"Now, what" learning occurred for you as a result of this shared experience? How will you apply what you learned to help you embrace beauty for ashes in your life? Use the reflection notes to respond.

Personal Reflection Notes:

_____
_____
_____
_____
_____
_____
_____
_____
_____
_____
_____
_____
_____
_____
_____
_____

I Forgive You

Chapter II
Perfect Love!

There is no love without forgiveness, and there is no forgiveness without love.
 -Bryant H. McGill, a Wall Street Journal and USA Today bestselling author, speaker, and activist in the fields of human potential and human rights.

"Love is patient, love is kind. It does not envy, it does not boast, it is not proud. It does not dishonor others, it is not self-seeking, it is not easily angered, it keeps no record of wrongs.
                                      - I Corinthians 13: 4-5 (NIV)

Jesus was the perfect example of the expression of God's love!

"But I tell you who hear me: Love your enemies, do good to those who hate you, bless those who curse you, pray for those who

> mistreat you. If someone strikes you on one cheek, turn to him the other also. If someone takes your cloak, do not stop him from taking your tunic. Give to everyone who asks you, and if anyone takes what belongs to you, do not demand it back. Do to others as you would have them do to you. If you love those who love you, what credit is that to you? Even sinners' love those who love them. And if you do good to those who are good to you, what credit is that to you? Even sinners' do that. And if you lend to those from whom you expect repayment, what credit is that to you? Even sinners lend to sinner, expecting to be repaid in full. But love your enemies, do good to them, lend to them without expecting to get anything back. Then your reward will be great, and you will be sons of the Most High, because he is kind to the ungrateful and wicked. Be merciful, just as your Father is merciful."
>
> \- Luke 6:27-36 (NIV)

Jesus is saying when you love those who treat you wrong, you are showing the mercy of God which is a manifestation of God's love. The sacrifice of Jesus Christ was the ultimate example of God's love for all humanity. God so loved the world that He gave Jesus Christ as an atoning sacrifice for the sins of the world.

It doesn't matter what people have said, what they have done, or what they continue to do! Jesus said,

Perfect Love

love them and do good! The key to releasing the blessings of God in your life is to follow the example that Jesus has set before us. Jesus forgave, Jesus loved, and Jesus prayed for his enemies. Whatever anger, resentment, or unforgiveness you may have in your heart, let it go! What you sow, is what you will reap! When you sow the seed of forgiveness, you will reap the harvest of forgiveness.

> **"…for whatever a man sows, this and this only is what he will reap."**
> -Galatians 6:7 (Amp)

Growing up, I would often hear people tell me that they loved me. The same individuals that told me they love me were the same individuals that inflicted emotional pain in my life, disappointment, and broken promises. Over time, vicarious learning took place based on my hearing and observing the behaviors. It wasn't long before I was repeating the vicious cycle of loving others based on my own self-serving and self-seeking interest. My mindset was simple, "seek to serve your own needs!" What I thought was love, was in fact the opposite of God's love. I learned how to love based on taking rather than giving. I witnessed firsthand family members taking advantage of me and my sibling's emotional state after the death of our parents. They stole priceless jewels, artifacts, and childhood pictures that we are attempting to retrieve this very day. The same people who said "I love you," were the exact same people who persecuted me for pursuing my dreams. The same people who said "I love you," were the same people who ridiculed my career choice. Like Joseph, the same people who said they loved me, despised me, became jealous of my accomplishments, and said I would never amount to anything in life. I began to take from everyone around me and it did not matter if their intentions were pure or not. As a result of my life experiences, my agenda was simple, "take advantage of others before they take advantage of me!" I realized after receiving Jesus into my heart that my acts of love were rooted in fear, hurt, and rejection. The love of God is "perfect love!" God never seeks to take, God seeks to give! The love of God is based on one question, **"How can I serve you?"**

God is Perfect Love!

What is Love?

- Love is patient!
- Love is kind!
- Love is not easily angered!
- Love keeps no record of wrongs!

Vine's Complete Expository Dictionary's definition of **Love**:
Love is the attitude of God toward His Son, (John 17:26); the human race, generally, (John 3:16; Romans 5:8); and to such as believe on the Lord Jesus

Perfect Love

Christ, particularly, (John 14:21); to convey His will to His children concerning their attitude one toward another, (John 13:34), and toward all men, (1Thessolonians. 3:12; I Corinthians 16:14; II Peter. 1:7); to express the essential nature of God, (I John 4:8). "Christian love has God for its primary object and expresses itself first of all in implicit obedience to His commandments, (John 14:15, 21, 23; 15:10; I John 2:5; 5:3; II John 6). "Christian love, whether exercised toward the brethren, or toward men generally, is not an impulse from the feelings, it does not always run with the natural inclinations, nor does it spend itself only upon those for whom some affinity is discovered. Love seeks the welfare of all, (Romans 15:2), and works no ill to any, (Romans13:8-10); love seeks opportunity to do good to 'all men, and especially toward them that are of the household of the faith.' (Galatians 6:10). See further (I Corinthians 13 and Colossians 3:12-14)."

~ God gave His Love as an example of how we should love each other! ~

"Beloved, let us (unselfishly) love and seek the best for one another, for love is from God; and everyone who loves (others) is born of God and knows God (through personal experience). The one who does not love has not become acquainted with God (does not and never did know Him), for God is love. (He is the originator of love, and it is an enduring

> **attribute of His nature.) By this the love of God was displayed in us, in that God has sent His (One and) only begotten Son (the One who is truly unique, the only One of His kind) into the world so that we might live through Him. In this is love, not that we loved God, but that He loved us and sent His son to be the propitiation (that is, the atoning sacrifice, and the satisfying offering) for our sins (fulfilling God's requirement for justice against sin and placating His wrath). Beloved, if God so loved us (in this incredible way), we also ought to love one another. No one has seen God at any time. But if we love one another (with unselfish concern), God abides in us, and His love (the love that is His essence abides in us."**
> - I John 4:7-12 (AMP)

Jesus was the manifestation of God's love for all humanity. John 3:16 (AMP), gives us a perfect illustration of the love of God in action on our behalf.

> **"For God so greatly loved and dearly prized the world that He (even) gave up His only begotten (unique) Son, so that whoever believes in (trusts in, clings to, relies on) Him shall not perish (come to destruction, be lost) but have eternal (everlasting) life.**

Everything that Jesus did was motivated by the love of God. Jesus went about doing good everywhere he went. He healed the sick. He feed the hungry. He raised the dead. He loved those who hated him. He forgave those who crucified him. God displayed His love for us in II Corinthians 5:21 (AMP) when He allowed Jesus to become that which he never committed--sin! **"For our sake He made Christ (virtually) to be sin Who knew no sin, so that in and through Him we might become (endued with, viewed as being in, and examples of) the righteousness of God (what we ought to be, approved and acceptable and in right relationship with Him, by His goodness)."** Jesus was the manifestation of God's love. Jesus came to heal, to forgive, to deliver, to prosper, to protect, and to restore our relationship with God. The love of God brings restoration to your life!

The love of God brings restoration to your life!

As a child, I had a lot of voids and personal insecurities. After the death of my parents, I struggled with anger and self-esteem issues. For a short period in my life, I battled with depression and suicidal ideation. I did not feel good about myself. I would pass by the mirror, never stopping because my reflection was a constant reminder of the hurt, pain, and brokenness I suffered after the passing of my parents. It was very difficult for me to express love towards anyone, and it was even more challenging for me to receive love because I had trust issues. Once I received Jesus into my heart, I realized that I never knew love because I did not understand God's love for me. The love of God is like a mirror, because it reflects to you the imperfections in your life yet, accepts you regardless of your shortcomings. The first thing I learned to do was to embrace myself. My daily routine was to visit the mirror first thing in the morning, look myself in the eyes and say, "God loves me just the way I am!" After doing this over a period of time, I began to see myself the way God saw me according to His word. I began to embrace God's love and this empowered me to express God's love towards others. The love of God brought restoration to my life and gave me a sense of purpose, passion, and meaning to live.

The love of God will make you whole, Nothing missing--Nothing broken!

Jesus came into this world not to condemn the world but to save the world. Jesus maximized every opportunity to display and extend the love of God to others. Jesus demonstrated through his ministry that the love of God was stronger than the counterfeit love that the devil tries to offer. The love of God has the power to deliver you out of the pit of unforgiveness.

Perfect Love will deliver and restore you to your rightful place!

God is love! Therefore, the nature of God is to love! The love of God is unconditional! The love of God never rejects, nor will it ever say, "you are not good

Perfect Love

enough!" The love of God will accept you in your broken state and your emotional baggage. Even when you turn away from God, He will never turn away from you. His nature is to love! Therefore, God will always love you and will never give up on you. The parable of the Lost Son is an excellent example of how God's love will restore your life.

> **"A certain man had two sons. The younger of them (inappropriately) said to his father, 'Father, give me the share of the property that falls to me.' So he divided the estate between them. A few days later, the younger son gathered together everything (that he had) and traveled to a distant country, and there he wasted his fortune in reckless and immoral living. Now when he had spent everything, a severe famine occurred in that country, and he began to do without and be in need. So he went and forced himself on one of the citizens of that country, who sent him into his fields to feed pigs. He would have gladly eaten the (carob) pods that the pigs were eating (but they could not satisfy his hunger), and no one was giving anything to him. But when he (finally) came to his senses, he said, 'How many of my father's hired men have more than enough food, while I am dying here of hunger! 'I will get up and go to my father, and I will say to him, "Father, I have sinned against heaven and in your sight. I am no longer worthy to be**

I Forgive You

called your son; (just) treat me like one of your hired men." So he got up and came to his father. But while he was still a long way off, his father saw him and was moved with compassion for him, and ran and embraced him and kissed him. And the son said to him, 'Father, I have sinned against heaven and in your sight; I am no longer worthy to be called your son.' But the father said to his servants, 'Quickly bring out the best robe (for the guest of honor) and put it on him; and give him a ring for his hand, and sandals for his feet. 'And bring the fattened calf and slaughter it, and let us (invite everyone and) feast and celebrate; for this son of mine was (as good as) dead and is alive again; he was lost and has been found. 'So they began to celebrate."

- Luke 15: 11-24 (AMP)

There are two very important points I would like make about this story:
1. The Lost Son represents you and me.
2. The father in the story is referring to God the Father. God is eagerly waiting and anticipating the time when we come to our senses and return to Him. He is waiting with open arms to embrace us, and restore us to our rightful place with Him!

After the death of my parents I felt abandoned, lost, hopeless, and insignificant. After I gave my heart to Jesus, God gave me two scriptures to assure me that

Perfect Love

He was my Father. Like the Lost Son, I was His son that was once dead, but now is alive--was once lost, but now is found!

> **"I will not leave you as orphans (comfortless, desolate, bereaved, forlorn, helpless); I will come (back) to you."**
>
> - John 14:18(Amp)

> **"Although my father and my mother have forsaken me, yet the Lord will take me up (adopt me as His child)."**
>
> - Psalms 27:10(Amp)

The Apostle Paul asks a very important question in Romans 8:35:

> **"Who shall ever separate us from Christ's love? Shall suffering, and affliction and tribulation? Or calamity and distress? Or persecution or hunger or destitution or peril or sword?"**

The Apostle Paul responds out of personal experience in Romans 8:39:

> **"Nor height nor depth, nor anything else in all creation will be able to separate us from the love of God which is in Christ Jesus our Lord."**

I Forgive You

The Apostle Paul is speaking from the position of someone who personally experienced the love of God firsthand. Paul was one of the most active natural enemies against the spread of the gospel of Jesus Christ. Paul's agenda before his conversion was one thing, "stop the spread of the gospel of Jesus Christ by all means necessary!" Paul was a modern-day terrorist! Paul spent his waking moments persecuting Christians until one day while on the road to Damascus, he had an encounter with Jesus Christ. The bible says the Jesus appeared and asked Saul, "why do you persecute me?" After Saul had his encounter with "perfect love," he eventually became The Apostle Paul and began to preach in the synagogues that Jesus is the Son of God! (Acts 9:1-20)

The love of God ignited a passion in the heart of Paul to share the love of God with the world. Paul no longer concerned himself with what he would eat or drink. He was not concerned about where he would sleep or his wellbeing! Paul took no care about what the situation looked like or any rumors about danger that awaited him. Paul had an encounter with "perfect love," therefore he had no FEAR! Paul had a revelation of the love of God. Paul realized that where there is love, there is no fear!

> **"There is no fear in love (dread does not exist). But perfect love (complete, full-grown) love drives out fear, because fear involves (the**

Perfect Love

expectation of divine) punishment, so the one who is afraid (of God's judgment) is not perfected in love (has not grown into a sufficient understanding of God's love).
– I John 4:18 (AMP)

Where there is LOVE…there is no fear!

I want to challenge everyone who is reading this book to make a decision to put away ALL fear in your life once and for all! Whatever God is calling you to do, just do it!
Repeat after me, No more fear!
F.E.A.R. or (**F**alse **E**vidence **A**ppearing **R**eal) comes from the devil!

"For God did not give us a spirit of timidity (of cowardice, of craven, and cringing and fawning fear), but (He has given us a spirit) of power and of love and of calm and well-balanced mind and discipline and self-control."
- 2 Timothy 1:7(Amp)

You were not designed to fear! You were designed to love! This is why your body undergoes so many adverse changes under the influence of fear. God gives you power through His love. The love of God will produce a calm and well-balanced mind. The mind is the battlefield and this is where satan launches his attack! If you think you can succeed or

I Forgive You

if you think you will fail, you are right! Why? The bible says in Proverbs 23:7

"For as he thinketh in his heart, so is he!"

Battles are won and lost in the mind! I submit to you that the very reason that Jesus Christ was so successful in ministry is because Jesus allowed the love of God to manifest the power that Jesus needed to maintain a calm and well-balanced mind. Therefore, when satan came to attack Jesus in his mind with the thoughts of fear, death, and embarrassment; Jesus was able to withstand satan's onslaught of evil suggestions. The love of God stabilized Jesus' mind and this allowed Jesus to maintain his focus and mission, "to seek and save that which was lost!"

The love of God brings stability to your thought life!

I want to deal with the spirit of fear right now with this simple prayer.
Repeat after me!

I speak to fear in the name of Jesus, and I command you to go from my life now! I rebuke the spirit of fear and break the power of fear off my life now in Jesus name! God did not give me a spirit of fear. God gave me a spirit of love, power, and well-balanced mind. I denounce fear now and I receive the love of God for my life now in Jesus name!

Amen! (Now, praise God for freedom from the spirit of fear!)

The Love of God gives freedom, focus, and faithfulness!

The love of God gives freedom, focus and faithfulness! As a result of the Apostle Paul being free, focused and faithful to the Lord Jesus Christ, he was able to fulfill his God given destiny. The love of God impacted Paul's life in such a way that he wrote these words in 1 Timothy 1:13-15;

> **"Even though I was formerly a blasphemer (of our Lord) and a persecutor (of His church) and a shameful and outrageous and violent aggressor (towards believers). Yet, I was shown mercy because I acted of ignorance in unbelief. The grace of our Lord (His amazing, unmerited favor and blessing) flowed out in superabundance (for me, together) with the faith and love which are (realized) in Christ Jesus. This is a faithful and trustworthy statement, deserving full acceptance and approval, that Christ Jesus came into the world to save sinners, among whom I am the foremost."**

I Forgive You

The Apostle Paul is saying that he was the worst sinner yet, Jesus Christ loved him and accepted him. Paul testifies that nothing can separate you from the love of God. Let me say it this way, there is nothing you can say or do that would change God's mind about you--God loves you!

Therefore; No Divorce, No Abuse, No Drug Addiction, No Lie, No Crime, No Sexual Sin, can separate you from the love of God!

The Apostle Paul's life is the perfect example of the power of God's love to win in every situation in life. The love of God literally changed Paul's life forever. Paul, went from Saul; a blasphemer and persecutor of the gospel of Jesus Christ to the Apostle Paul; an advocate of the gospel of Jesus Christ.

"The love of God is our power to win in every situation in life!"

The Greatest Commandment!

"Hearing that Jesus had silenced the Saducees, the Pharisees got together. One of them, an expert in the law, tested him with this question: "Teacher, which is the greatest commandment in the Law?" "Jesus replied: "Love the Lord your God with all your heart and with all your soul and with all your mind. This is the first and greatest commandment. And the second is

Perfect Love

like it: Love your neighbor as yourself. All the Law and the Prophets hang on these two commandments."

- Matthew. 22:34-40 (NIV)

When we love God, we learn from God's love how to love ourselves. When we learn to love ourselves the way God loves us, we are able to love others with the love of God. I tried to love others without the love of God. The end result was always disastrous! What I did not know then was that Matthew 22:34-40 reveals the formula for successful relationships, (marriage, family, friends, colleagues, ministry, and business) is LOVE.

Love is first! Love is key! Love is the very source of life! Love gives life, and love drives out fear! Love was the foundation and the reason that Jesus experienced unlimited power in the miracles he performed yesterday, today and forever! This is why Jesus, said in Matthew 22:37-39, "Love the Lord your God with all your heart and with all your soul and with all your mind. Afterwards, Love your neighbor as yourself."

"This is the message you heard from the beginning: We should love one another. Do not be like Cain, who belonged to the evil one and murdered his brother. And why did he murder him? Because his own actions were evil and his brother's were righteous."

I Forgive You

-1 John 3:11-12 (NIV)

"Dear friends, let us love one another, for love comes from God. Everyone who loves has been born of God and knows God. Whoever does not love does not know God, because God is love. This is how God showed his love among us: He sent his one and only Son into the world that we might live through him. This is love: not that we loved God, but that he loved us and sent his Son as an atoning sacrifice for our sin. Dear friends, since God so loved us, we also ought to love one another. No one has ever seen God; but if we love one another, God lives in us and his love is made complete in us."
-1 John 4:7-12 (NIV)

The pyramid represents the flow of the love of God. The foundation of love is God, **"Love the Lord your God with all your heart, soul and mind."** The next

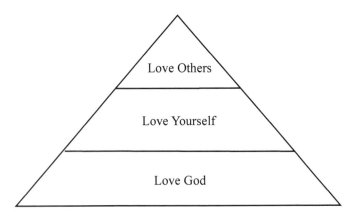

Matthew 22:37-39

Perfect Love

level of love is to **"love yourself." "the final level of love "is to love others."**
The most powerful level of your love walk and I believe the most dangerous to the kingdom of darkness and satan's plans of destruction is when you can outwardly display **"the love of God for your neighbor as yourself."**

I believe that everything we do in life is either motivated by love or hate. I submit to you that the answer the problems of the world today is the love of God!

God is love! Therefore, everything that He does is rooted in love. Paul made a strong case that love is a necessity for life.

> **"If I speak in the tongues of men and of angels, but have not love, I am only a resounding gong or a clanging cymbal. If I have the gift of prophecy and can fathom all mysteries and all knowledge, and if I have a faith that can move mountains, but have not love, I am nothing. If I give all I possess to the poor and surrender my body to the flames, but have not love, I gain nothing." "Love is patient, love is kind. It does not envy, it does not boast, it is not proud. It is not rude, it is not self-seeking, it is not easily angered, it keeps no record of wrongs. Love does not delight in evil but rejoices with the truth. It always protects, always trusts,**

I Forgive You

always hopes, always perseveres." "Love never fails. But where there are prophecies, they will cease; where there are tongues, they will be stilled; where there is knowledge, it will pass away. For we know in part and we prophesy in part, but when perfection comes, the imperfect disappears. When I was a child, I talked like a child. When I became a man, I put childish ways behind me. Now we see but a poor reflection as in a mirror; then we shall see face to face. Now I know in part; then I shall know fully, even as I am fully known." "And now these three remain: faith, hope and love. But the greatest of these is love!"

-1 Corinthians 13:1-13 (NIV)

"Forgiveness is the final form of love." - Reinhold Niebuhr

The love of God empowers you to pray for your enemies. (Matthew 5:44)
The love of God gives you peace of mind to endure the storms of life. (Philippians 4:7)
The love of God gives you joy and strength to stand in mist of sorrow. (Nehemiah 8:10)
The love of God empowers you to do good no matter how others treat you. (Luke 6:35)
The love of God gives you the power to forgive. (Colossians 3:13)
The love of God is perfect love. (John 13:1)

Perfect Love

The love of God is patient, kind, it's not rude, it's not easily angered and it keeps no record of wrongs! The Love of God is Perfect Love and Perfect Love Never Fails!

Chapter II: Perfect Love

Key Principles
- God is Love!
- The nature of love is to give.
- Jesus was the perfect expression of God's love.
- The love of God gives you value, worth and purpose!
- Nothing can separate you from the love of God!
- Perfect love drives out fear!
- Love is The Greatest Commandment!

Meditation Scriptures:
John 3:16 (Amp)
"For God so greatly loved and dearly prized the world that He (even) gave up His only begotten (unique) Son, so that whoever believes in (trusts in, clings to, relies on) Him shall not perish (come to destruction, be lost) but have eternal (everlasting) life. (Amp)

II Corinthians 5:21 (Amp)
For our sake He made Christ (virtually) to be sin Who knew no sin, so that in and through Him we might become (endued with, viewed as being in, and examples of) the righteousness of God (what we ought to be, approved and acceptable and in right relationship with Him, by His goodness).

Perfect Love

II Timothy 1:7 (Amp)
"For God did not give us a spirit of timidity (of cowardice, of craven, and cringing and fawning fear), but (He has given us a spirit) of power and of love and of calm and well-balanced mind and discipline and self-control."

I John 4:7-12 (NIV)
"Dear friends, let us love one another, for love comes from God. Everyone who loves has been born of God and knows God. Whoever does not love does not know God, because God is love. This is how God showed his love among us: He sent his one and only Son into the world that we might live through him. This is love: not that we loved God, but that he loved us and sent his Son as an atoning sacrifice for our sin. Dear friends, since God so loved us, we also ought to love one another. No one has ever seen God; but if we love one another, God lives in us and his love is made complete in us." -1

I John 4:18
"There is no fear in love (dread does not exist). But perfect love (complete, full-grown) love drives out fear, because fear involves (the expectation of divine) punishment, so the one who is afraid (of God's judgment) is not perfected in love (has not grown into a sufficient understanding of God's love).

Chapter II: Reflection Questions

Define love in your own words and describe how you display acts of love towards other people.

_____
_____
_____
_____
_____
_____
_____
_____

Reflect on a time when you were offended. Describe the nature of the offense. How did you learn to love the individual that offended you? What was the most challenging aspect of this process for you?

_____
_____
_____
_____
_____
_____
_____
_____
_____
_____

Perfect Love

The writer says, "the love of God is our power to win in every situation in life!" What does this mean to you? Why is God's love the prerequisite to obtain power to overcome hurt, offense, and ultimately, walk in forgiveness?

_____
_____
_____
_____
_____
_____
_____
_____

As you reflect on the chapter, and some of the personal information that the author shared about his life experiences, ask yourself the following questions:

- **What?**
- **So, what?**
- **Now, what?**

Begin with defining and sharing **"what"** facts and events the author shared in the chapter, *Perfect Love.*

"So, what" did you learn about yourself as a result of what the author shared?

I Forgive You

"Now, what" learning occurred for you as a result of this shared experience? How will you apply what you learned to help you embrace God's perfect love? Use the reflection notes to respond.

Personal Reflection Notes:

_____
_____
_____
_____
_____
_____
_____
_____
_____
_____
_____
_____
_____
_____
_____
_____
_____
_____
_____
_____
_____
_____
_____

Perfect Love

I Forgive You

Chapter III
Offense Will Come!

"We should be too big to take offense and too noble to give it." - Abraham Lincoln, 16th U.S. President

At one time or another, offense will come into your life! You will have an opportunity to become offended by something that was done directly or indirectly to you. **Offense** is defined by the *Webster 1828 American Dictionary* as "any transgression of law, divine or human; a crime; sin; act of wickedness or omission of duty."

Someone will transgress the law against you; commit a crime against you, sin against you, or act in omission of duty when it is in their power to respond in your favor. I can recall countless situations when I was treated unjust, lied on, falsely accused of something I didn't do, set up to fail, and misunderstood. What I discovered in every situation

I Forgive You

when offense came, it didn't matter if it was a family member; friend, co-worker, spouse, or child--the end result was the same; hurt, pain, disappointment, resentment, and unforgiveness. Offense is dangerous because of the toxicity that comes as a result of the constant rehearsal of the pain and disappointment. I've learned that you can't do anything about your past. However, if you choose to forgive you not only free yourself of your past, you position yourself to receive God's will for your future.

"Stop watering things that were never meant to grow in your life."
  T.D. Jakes, pastor, author, filmmaker, and Bishop of The Potter's House, a Nondenominational American megachurch

When you meditate on the offenses in your life, your thoughts are like seeds that are watered (feed and nourished) by your words. The more you talk about the offenses, the more water and nourishment you provide for the seeds to grow in your heart. It shouldn't be a surprise to you that five, ten, fifteen, or twenty years later, you are still struggling and dealing with the same past hurts, disappointments, pain, and resentment. The reason is simple, you've watered things in your heart that were never meant to grow in your life! Jesus taught in Luke 6:27-35, how to we should respond when the seed of offense has been sown in your garden (heart) to assure that we are not

Offence Will Come

watering thoughts that was never meant to grow into manifestation in our lives.

> *"But I say to you who hear (Me and pay attention to My words): Love (that is unselfishly seek the best or higher good for) your enemies, (make it a practice to) do good to those who hate you, bless and show kindness to those who curse you, pray for those who mistreat you. Whoever strikes you on the cheek, offer him the other one also (simply ignore insignificant insults or losses and do not bother to retaliate-maintain your dignity). Whoever takes away your coat, do not withhold your shirt from him either. Give to everyone who asks of you. Whoever takes away yours, do not demand it back. Treat others the same way you want them to treat you. If you (only) love those who love you, what credit is that to you? For even sinners love those who love them. If you do good to those who do good to you, what credit is that to you? For even sinners do the same. If you lend (money) to those from whom you expect to receive (it back), what credit is that to you? Even sinners lend to sinners expecting to receive back the same amount. But love (that is unselfishly seek the best or higher good for) your enemies, and do good, and lend, expecting nothing in return; for your reward will be great (rich, abundant), and you will be sons of the Most High; because He Himself is kind and gracious and good to the*

ungrateful and the wicked. Be merciful (responsive, compassionate, tender) just as your (heavenly) Father is merciful."

– Luke 6:27-35 (AMP)

Jesus is saying that it doesn't matter what offense was given, we should always respond with love and repay good for evil. That is a long way from man's retaliatory nature expressed as such: "if you hurt me, I'll hurt you back!" and "If you do me wrong, I will never forgive you!" It's not a matter of if offense comes--because offense will come into your life. It's a matter of how you respond to the offense. President Lincoln was absolutely right when he said we should be too big to take offense and too noble to give it. I believe somewhere in President Lincoln's life, he was offended, but he got hold of the teachings of Jesus Christ and he learned from the Bible the dangers of taking offense and offending others. The Bible says when we unselfishly love and seek the best for each other, there is no occasion for stumbling or offense.

"The one who loves and unselfishly seeks the best for his (believing) brother lives in the light and in him there is no occasion for stumbling or offense (he does not hurt the cause of Christ or lead others to sin)."

– 1 John 2:10

It's not the Offense…it's how you respond to the Offense!

Offence Will Come

> ***"Blessed (anticipating God's presence, spiritually mature) are the pure in heart (those with integrity, moral courage, and godly character) for they will see God"***
> - Matthew 5:8 (AMP)

I would like to say it this way, blessed are the pure in heart, who refuses to take offense for they will see God's will manifested in their lives! When offense comes, you have to make a choice to either accept the offense or reject the offense.

> **"Blessed (joyful, spiritually favored) is he who does not take offense..."**
> – Luke 7:23 (AMP)

I believe in the life of Joseph, he understood the danger and consequences of offending other people and allowing himself to take offense. Joseph had a "pure" heart and the scripture doesn't give an account of Joseph taking offense even when retribution appeared to be justifiable. I believe God was able to bless Joseph to the degree that He blessed him because Joseph maintained a pure heart regardless of how people lied on him or mistreated him. Joseph maintained his integrity, moral courage, and godly character. Joseph's vision was bigger than any offense! I want you to know that what God has placed on the inside of you is bigger than any offense the devil can dish out! Focus on the product (your vision) and go through the process (the journey) to obtain your vision!

"Focus on **The Product** and go through **The Process!**"

If Joseph allowed his brothers' offenses coupled with the lying accusations of Potiphar's wife to set up in his heart, he would have become bitter and sought revenge for himself instead of allowing God to avenge him. Joseph would have forfeited God's plan for his life which was to stand in the gap for his family and to address the global economic crisis during his time as a world leader.

> ***"Man looks at the outward appearance, but the Lord looks at the heart."***
>
> -1 Samuel 16:7(AMP)

When we are experiencing challenging moments in our lives, we tend to cover up our emotional scares and dress up our pain. We become professional pretenders to protect our outward appearance, but God examines the heart! God looks at our heart because He judges the matters of the heart. If Joseph would have succumbed to his feelings, God would have seen beyond Joseph's fine clothing, eloquent speech, and majestic image to see that his heart was filled with anger, rage, resentment, bitterness, unforgiveness, malice, strife, and revenge. Therefore, God would not have been able to trust Joseph with the

Offence Will Come

wealth, power, influence, and authority of Egypt. Joseph would have been a modern day evil dictator who would eventually abuse his power and misuse his influence. It's a known fact that "hurting people hurt people." Joseph's focus would have been his own agenda instead of God's agenda. Money, power, and influence magnifies what's in your heart. If you are a vindictive, spiteful, vengeful person, money will magnify that behavior and give you the platform to carry out the matters of your heart. God will not promote a person who has a heart filled with bitterness and revenge because **God does not bless mess!** God will bless people who have a pure heart filled with integrity, moral courage, and godly character. Joseph had a pure heart therefore, God was able to trust him.

Can God Trust You?

If God can trust you, He will give you more because He sees that your heart is pure and you can be trusted to do the right thing no matter how others treat you. The motivation in your heart would be to please God! I remember early on in my Christian journey when I gave my life to Jesus on the campus of Eastern Illinois University, I wanted to be a blessing to everyone I encountered. I would give away clothing, volunteer to feed the homeless, and encouraging people on a daily basis. After returning back to Chicago, I received a prophetic word from a local church I was visiting with profound clarity. I heard

I Forgive You

God clearly say to me, He could trust me because my heart was pure and I had a genuine concern for the welfare of other people. God would use me to lead, encourage, motivate, inspire, and empower others to identify and pursue their purpose in life. Years later, while working as a school counselor, the Lord gave me and my wife the vision for Teen-Train, which is our community faith-based organization. Teen-Train emphasizes programming around mentoring, leadership training, college and career readiness, community service, conflict resolution skills, self-esteem, goal setting, and summer enrichment programs to help youth and families.

It is very important for you to understand that you can't allow offense to stop the plan of God from manifesting in your life. God is a God of purpose and when He created you and I, He placed purpose on the inside of us. God placed something inside of you that is special, unique, and bigger than you! God created every person with a uniquely designed specific assignment to be carried out so that other people would be blessed as a result of your obedience to God. Your purpose is never about you! It's about what God can do in you and through you if you don't allow offense to stop you!

If I would have allowed the offenses I experienced in my childhood after the death of my parents to continue to grow in my life, it would have negatively impacted my vision about family, my assignment, and my purpose. Because I opened myself up to God's will for my life, He has opened many doors of opportunities for me to speak at schools, colleges/universities, weddings, workshops, conferences, and panel discussions around various topics related to marriage, leadership, and purpose. Like Joseph, the vision that God showed me was coming to pass in my life as I continued to grow in my understanding of God's love and continued to pass off offense daily.

"Offense cuts you off from God. We separate ourselves from the pipeline. I've never seen anything block blessings from Heaven except offense."
  - John Bevere, Christian Author and internationally sought-after speaker

The greatness that God has placed on the inside of each and every person individually and collectively has the power to change the world if we keep our hearts pure and live a life of integrity, moral courage, and godly character. The Bible says in Romans 8:19 (AMP)

> *"For (even the whole) creation (all nature) waits eagerly for the children of God to be revealed."*

This scripture tells me that it is extremely important for God's people to grow up and stop getting offended! Romans 8:19 specifically talks about mental, emotional, and spiritual "maturity" that comes from being fully submitted to God's will and allowing God to manifest His glory through our acts of obedience to His word.

> *"Behold, to obey is better that sacrifice..."*
> - 1Samuel 15:22 (AMP)

Your decision to obey God's word will produce the results that God promised to bring to pass in your life. I made the decision to obey God when He told me to forgive. As a result of my obedience, God brought to pass the things He promised me. However, if I would have made the decision to disobey God and handle the situations and relationships in my life out of my own unresolved hurt and rejection, I would have forfeited God's will and further perpetuated the vicious cycle of hurting others people. Obeying God will allow God to do great and mighty works in your life like He did in the life of Joseph. I would like for you to pray this simple prayer to keep your heart pure to receive God's will in your life:

> **"Lord, keep my heart pure so You can use me to fulfill Your will in the earth. I submit to Your will for my life and I desire for You to use me for Your glory. I release all offense and I repent for every time I have offended others. Keep me forgiving with You and forgiving others in Jesus Name!"**

Offence Will Come

It is amazing how God strategically planted and elevated Joseph to become second in charge of Egypt. Most people would love to have Joseph's ending without his beginning. In other words, they want the end **"PRODUCT"** of leadership, influence, wealth, and fame without going through the **"PROCESS,"** of maturing spiritually, mentally, and emotionally. The process and the product are one in the same and you can't have one without the other. You have to learn how to deal with shame, anger, disgrace, and offense because this is part of the process to achieve greatness. Luke 12:48 (AMP) says,

> **"From everyone to whom much has been given, much will be required; and to whom they entrusted much, of him they ask all the more."**

In other words, the more success you experience the more offenses you will encounter. I personally believe the degree that you can handle offense will determine the degree God can trust you. It's not the offense, it's your response to the offense that counts in the eyes of God!

When I think about offense, I think about a sink that has a slow drain. If the slow drain is never addressed, it will eventually become a clogged pipe. That clogged pipe can lead to more expensive repairs in your home. The same thing happens in the life of a person when offense grows into bitterness and

I Forgive You

unforgiveness. The bitterness and unforgiveness in your heart is like the slow drain that will eventually become clogged. Once, your heart becomes clogged, the flow of God's word and His blessings in your life will stop and this could lead to more serious complex life issues. Think about the time when Jesus visited his hometown and the hearts of the people were clogged to the degree that Jesus couldn't work any miracles on their behalf.

> *"Jesus left there and came to His hometown (Nazareth); and His disciples followed Him. When the Sabbath came, He began to teach in the synagogue; and many who listened to Him were astonished, saying, "Where did this man get these things (this knowledge and spiritual insight)? What is this wisdom (this confident understanding of the Scripture) that has been given to Him, and such miracles as these performed by His hands? Is this not the carpenter, the son of Mary, and the brother of James and Joses and Judas and Simon? Are His sisters not here with us? And they were (deeply) offended by Him (and their disapproval blinded them to the fact that He was anointed by God as the Messiah). Jesus said to them, "A prophet is not without honor (respect) except in his hometown and among his relatives and his own household." And He could not do a miracle there at all (because of their unbelief) except*

Offence Will Come

that He laid hands on a few sick people and healed them."
– Mark 6:1-5 (AMP)

Their position of offense fostered an atmosphere of unbelief which stifled the anointing to work miracles. If you allow offense to clog up your heart, you set yourself up for the following processes to take place in your life:

- Unbelief
- Contaminated faith
- Stifled anointing
- Limited access to God's miracle working power

What I find interesting in the text of Mark 6:1-5, is that Jesus who was God in the flesh had unlimited power yet, could not perform a miracle because of unbelief. All of this was due to the fact that the people were "deeply offended" by Him teaching on the Sabbath! It did not matter what Jesus believed or knew He could do for the people. What mattered was that the people took "offense" and as a result of their position, unbelief stopped the flow of miracles from manifesting in their lives.

I Forgive You

Matthew 9:29 (AMP), is an example of how important faith is when it comes to activating the power of God in your life.

"Then He touched their eyes, saying, "According to your faith (your trust and confidence in My power and My ability to heal) it will be done to you."

Offense comes to contaminate your faith and to stop the delivering power of God on your behalf. Always remember, offense leads to bitterness, bitterness leads to resentment, resentment leads to unforgiveness, and unforgiveness leads to failure in LIFE!

How Do You Deal with Offense?

The way you respond to offense will determine the level of success you will experience in your life. Offense hinders personal, spiritual, professional, and emotional growth. It is important to understand that offense blocks your ability to grow forward in life. This is why the scripture warns us about the dangers of offense. I recommend that you consider the following steps when dealing with offense:

1. **Learn from the Offense:**
   - What happened?
   - What did you learn about yourself as a result of the experience?

- How will you respond differently when offense comes again?

2. **<u>Release the Offense:</u>**
   - Understand that offense will come.
   - Understand that offense stops your forward progress.
   - Understand that offense fosters unbelief, contaminates your faith, stifles the anointing, and limits your ability to receive God's will for your life.
   - Understand that offense will clog your heart.
   - Pray Psalms 51 when you feel offended.

3. **<u>Grow Forward from the Offense:</u>**
   - Remember that hurting people hurt people!
   - Focus on the Product and go through the Process!
   - When you forgive the person who offended you, you become empowered!

Forgiveness is about empowering yourself, rather than empowering your past.

-T. D. Jakes, <u>pastor, author, filmmaker, and Bishop of The Potter's House, a Nondenominational megachurch</u>

I Forgive You

I have learned from personal experience that every time offense has come into my life, I had the opportunity to either grow forward, or remain stagnant. In most cases, I missed the opportunity to grow due to the fact that I did not understand God's word, nor did I understand God's will for my life. After coming to know Jesus as my Lord and Savior, I learned the key to growing forward was first making a decision to forgive then, purposely thinking positive thoughts about my situation.

> ***"Finally, brothers and sisters, whatever is true, whatever is noble, whatever is right, whatever is pure, whatever is lovely, whatever is admirable… if anything is excellent or praiseworthy…think about such things."***
> - Philippians 4:8 (AMP),

I became empowered as I learned to replace negative thoughts with positive thoughts. I learned to focus my energy, time, and attention on the fact that God loves me and with God all things become possible. **ALL THINGS ARE POSSIBLE!**

The benefits of releasing offense:
1. You maintain a clean and pure heart.
2. You free yourself from your past.
3. God can bless you.
4. You empower yourself.
5. God can trust you.

Offence Will Come

When offense comes, it's an opportunity for you grow. When offense comes, it's an opportunity for you to trust God. When offense comes, it's and opportunity for you to see the salvation of the Lord!

What was meant for evil or to bring destruction to your life, God will use for your personal and spiritual growth and development.

> *"Blessed (anticipating God's presence, spiritually mature) are the pure in heart (those with integrity, moral courage, and godly character) for they will see God"*
>
> - Matthew 5:8 (AMP)

Chapter III: Offense Will Come

Key Principles
- **Offense Will Come!**
- **STOP watering things that were not meant to grow in your life!**
- **Focus on The Product and go through The Process!**
- **Man looks at the outward appearance but God looks at the heart!**
- **Offense leads to unbelief which hinders the power of God in your life.**
- **Offense presents the opportunity to Grow Forward!**
- **With God, ALL THINGS ARE POSSIBLE!**

Meditation Scriptures:
I John 2:10
"The one who loves and unselfishly seeks the best for his (believing) brother lives in the light and in him there is no occasion for stumbling or offense (he does not hurt the cause of Christ or lead others to sin)."

Matthew 5:8
"Blessed (anticipating God's presence, spiritually mature) are the pure in heart (those with integrity, moral courage, and godly character) for they will see God"

I Samuel 16:7
"Man looks at the outward appearance, but the Lord looks at the heart."

I Samuel 15:22
"Behold, to obey is better that sacrifice."

Philippians 4:8
"Finally, brothers and sisters, whatever is true, whatever is noble, whatever is right, whatever is pure, whatever is lovely, whatever is admirable…if anything is excellent or praiseworthy…think about such things."

Chapter III: Reflection Questions

The writer says that offense is a seed, and your words are the water that feeds and nourishes the seed. What seed(s) of offense are you watering on a daily basis? Briefly describe the unresolved hurt that you find yourself constantly rehearsing with your words?

_____
_____
_____
_____
_____
_____
_____
_____

Focus on the **Product** and go through the **Process**! Explain in your own words why this is important. Why is it difficult to focus on the product (deliverance from offense) while going through the Process (dealing with the hurt from the offense)?

_____
_____
_____
_____
_____
_____

Offence Will Come

When offense sets up in your heart, it causes the following processes to take place in your life:

1. _____
2. _____
3. _____
4. _____

What are the 3 ways to deals with offense?

1. _____
2. _____
3. _____

As you reflect on the chapter, and some of the personal information that the author shared about his life experiences, ask yourself the following questions:

- **What?**
- **So, what?**
- **Now, what?**

I Forgive You

Begin with defining and sharing **"what"** facts and events the author shared in the chapter, *Offense Will Come*.

"So, what" did you learn about yourself as a result of what the author shared?

"Now, what" learning occurred for you as a result of this shared experience? How will you apply what you learned to help you understand that offense will come, and how to appropriately respond when offended? Use the reflection notes to respond.

Personal Reflection Notes:

_____
_____
_____
_____
_____
_____
_____
_____
_____
_____
_____
_____
_____
_____

Offence Will Come

I Forgive You

Chapter IV
Faith To Forgive

"If your brother or sister sins against you, rebuke them; and if they repent, forgive them. Even if they sin against you seven times in a day and seven times come back to you saying 'I repent,' you must forgive them." The apostles said to the Lord, "Increase our faith!"
- Luke 17:3-5 (NIV)

When I first read this verse of scripture my first thought was the concept of forgiving is going to be a very difficult and challenging process. My rationale for this position was based on the fact that we naturally don't want people to think our decision to forgive them is an indication of weakness. Our natural defense mechanism is to get angry, bitter, resentful, and develop a grudge if left unresolved or unaddressed. We continue with a mindset that we need to hold on to the hurt as experience to help educate us about people and to guide us in the way we should act moving forward with others. In some cases, we hold on to the memory of past hurt in order to establish and maintain boundaries as a form of self-preservation when interacting with people. In most cases, we just think the offender doesn't deserve to be forgiven. So, we justify our position not to forgive to maintain some sense of control and power, and to remove the perception that we are weak. However, I like what Bishop T.D. Jakes said, **"We think that forgiveness is weakness, but it's absolutely not; it takes a very strong person to forgive."**

Forgiveness is not a position of the Weak…it's a position of the Strong!

Reflecting on the scripture in Luke 17:3-5, I believe Jesus's disciples were challenged daily with some of the same struggles we deal with when encountering offense in our lives. I believe like Peter posed the question in Matthew 18:21-22, most of us would have asked Jesus the same question for clarification purposes,

> *"Lord, how many times shall I forgive my brother and sister who sins against me? Up to seven times?" Jesus answered, "I tell you, not seven times, but seventy times."*

Jesus replied to Peter, "not seven times, but seventy times!" I believe Jesus said "seventy times" because forgiveness is an ongoing process and our position and decision to forgive must be unwavering and consistently consistent! In other words, it doesn't matter who lied on you, stole from you, hurt you, caused you grief, pain, or sorrow--you have to forgive! God expects you and I to keep forgiving people over, and over, and over again because He keeps forgiving you and I over, and over, and over again.

> ***"Keep us forgiven with you and forgiving others."***
>
> - Luke 11:4 (MSG Bible)

Strength is required to forgive, because what we feel and what we experience is real! The hurt, rejection, anger, and bitterness are real feelings. Strength is required to withstand the emotional pressure, enabling you to resist the urge to give up and quit on life. I recall a very painful time in my life when I was dealing with deep hurt and rejection from a past relationship. The individual continued to do things intentionally to demean, degrade, embarrass, and provoke me. Initially, I didn't understand why the individual continued to expend so much time and energy to inflict pain and discomfort in my life. Later, I realized that hurting people hurt people. The emotional pressure was building daily, and I wanted to lash out and retaliate. I remember seeking the Lord in prayer about what I should do and how I should handle the situation. The Lord spoke to me,

I Forgive You

"Dwayne, you have to forgive!" My response was, "I'm tired of my name being scandalized, my kindness being taking for weakness, and the ongoing attempts to sabotage my life!" The Lord responded, "forgiveness is not a position of the weak, it's a position of the strong. Forgiveness is for you and has nothing to do with the offender. You cannot forgive in your own strength because it is not possible. You must have faith to receive my strength to forgive. You can do "ALL" things through Christ (the Anointed One and His anointing) who strengthens you Dwayne… now forgive!" At that moment, I realized my decision to not forgive would cost me more than I was willing to pay. The light affliction I was going through, although it seemed like an eternity in my life, was not worth forfeiting the assignment God had for my future.

At that time in my life, I needed additional income to address some financial deficits. I remember while praying to the Lord for direction, the Lord began to press upon my heart the need to forgive people from both my past and present who hurt me. After making a decision by faith to forgive, God began to move in my life and opened a door of opportunity for me to work as a part-time counselor at an all-male youth residential treatment center. In this position, I worked with youth who had criminal backgrounds and ongoing substance abuse issues. The center offered weekly Alcoholic Anonymous meetings and other support services to help with sobriety, anger management, coping skills, and life-skills. There were countless times I wanted to quit because of the emotional and physical drain from dealing with my own personal issues. However, I continued to remain faithful to the assignment and I maintained a positive attitude no matter what was going on in my personal life. While facilitating my groups, I could see and hear the unresolved hurt, pain, rejection, bitterness, and grudges that the youth in the center expressed both verbally and non-verbally. The unresolved hurt was eating away at these young men, and because they lacked the knowledge and understanding of how to cope with the pain, the outward manifestations was the risky behaviors and acts of violence towards self and others. God gave me favor with the staff and the clients. They began to seek out my weekly groups because they felt the positive energy and authentic love. During my groups, I would often challenge the clients to love life and seek new opportunities to restore broken relationships. There was no such thing as a nine-to-five schedule for me. I would leave the center at midnight physically exhausted. However, the compassion I felt for those young men motivated me to be faithful and diligent with this new assignment God had entrusted to me. I could clearly see the clients needed hope and peace that could only come through a relationship with Jesus Christ. The challenge became, how do I get this message to the clients? The center received state funding, and as a result they did not allow "religious" services on the premises. However, with God all things are possible.

I Forgive You

I prayed, "Lord, if you open the door, I'll preach Your gospel!" It wasn't two weeks after that prayer that the director of the center pulled me into the office and said, "Dwayne, the behaviors in the house have been completely out of control! We know that the clients enjoy your groups, but we need more to offer them. Would you be willing to run a weekly "spirituality" group? She went on to say, "I don't care what you do, just do what you do because they seem to respond to you in a positive way!" At that moment, my mouth dropped and I gladly accepted the opportunity to facilitate the "spirituality" group. This really upset the devil because he not only turned up the attacks in my life, he made sure the "spirituality" group had a scheduling conflict (same time, same day) as the weekly AA Meetings. The AA meetings were mandatory sessions the clients were required to attend in order to acquire sponsors and remain in compliance with their treatment goals. I went home and prayed to God for the weekly messages, and I relied on the Holy Spirit to lead me. It was a total of thirty-nine youth residing in the residential center. I had about twelve guys attend my first "spirituality" group out of curiosity. God showed up and showed out! The message of hope, love, and purpose was ministered and the youth embraced it. They did not want the group to end. I had clients coming up to me before bedtime hours asking for prayer. I was totally amazed at what God did in that group. Each week my group grew larger and larger until thirty-eight out of thirty-nine of the youth were in attendance faithfully for

Faith To Forgive

"spirituality" group. The AA meetings had to be rescheduled because all the students wanted to attend my group instead of the AA meetings. To accommodate the request of the clients, and make sure each client was on track with their treatment goals, the schedule was modified. God was showing me that through my act of obedience to forgive by faith, He was able to not only bless my life, but bless the lives of the youth in that treatment center. God was definitely doing something special in both me and the clients simultaneously. My relationship with God grew deeper and my faith became stronger and stronger. My weekly "spirituality" group became the single most popular group in the entire center. God gave me favor with the director like God gave Joseph favor with Potiphar.

My church, Living Word Christian Center, would have routine Men's Fellowship Services to develop the men spiritually and give them strategies to cope with the pressures of everyday life. I decided to ask the director for permission to take the entire house to a men's fellowship that was being held at my church. She granted my request and allowed me to utilize the company vans to transport all the youth to the men's fellowship event. This was a great experience for the youth because they met positive strong men that looked like them and had similar life experiences. We had dinner and listened as Dr. Bill Winston, <u>American preacher, author, visionary leader, and business entrepreneur</u> taught on the subject of

I Forgive You

manhood and purpose. The young men were publicly recognized by Dr. Winston and encouraged to visit again. Their lives were positively impacted forever because they experienced the power of God's love without prejudice. I recall speaking with the youth after the event, and every last one of them personally thanked me, and sought me out for prayer when they had court dates, weekend passes, or family visits to assure that everything would go well. It became evident God was using me in a mighty way to impact those young men. I recall one particular client asking me to pray a prayer of protection over him for his upcoming weekend pass. He informed me that he had received some death threats, and he was really concerned about his safety. However, he missed his family, and was willing to risk his safety in order to visit with them. I prayed a very specific prayer of protection over him and asked God to reveal the plans of the enemy and to protect him from any hidden traps that would endanger his life. I went on about my business because I prayed in faith, and I believed God for his safe return. When I returned to work the following week, the young man ran up to me full of excitement and gratitude. He said, "Dwayne, thank you for praying for me!" "God is real and He protected me just like you prayed!" He informed me that while he was on his weekend pass, an old girlfriend reached out to him and requested to see him. He was excited to hear from her. They had a prior relationship and their interaction ended on good terms. He shared with me that he agreed to meet her

Faith To Forgive

later that evening. He hung up the phone and walked away to get himself dressed. However, something un-explainable happened. The phone call somehow did not disconnect. In-stead, the call defaulted from the head-set to speaker mode. What he heard next was a very disturbing conversation. The young woman was talking with rival gang members about their plans to draw him out of hiding because they had been looking for him to kill him. The young man listened intently. Detail by detail the plan and plot to kill him unfolded—but this was one trap he would not fall into. He was covered by God because I prayed he would not fall into any of the enemy's traps. In an instant he remembered the prayer for him and how God honored that prayer. He was totally stunned, and speechless all at once. If that phone would not have miraculously defaulted from the headset to speaker phone, he would have been another homicide reported on the local evening news. The client was some amazed, grateful, and appreciative that God spared his life. Needless to say, he told everyone in the house and I started to receive prayer requests for legal issues, restored relationships, and protection. As a result of the testimonies and the successful "spirituality" groups all the young men at the center received prayer and accepted Jesus into their hearts. The staff would share with me how the disputes between the youth in the house decreased significantly, behaviors were improving daily, relationships with family members were being restored, treatment goals achieved, and clients were

I Forgive You

successfully discharging out of the treatment program. I would leave the treatment center after finishing my "spirituality" group feeling refreshed and rejuvenated. It was such a great feeling to see the youth empowered, excited, and seeking God for purpose and destiny.

I made a decision to forgive by faith and to trust God for His strength to forgive my enemies. Not only did God lead me to scriptures to build my faith to forgive, He was able to show His love through my obedience and touch the lives of thirty-nine hurting and lost young men. My decision to forgive by faith clearly allowed me to see that what the devil meant for my destruction (anger), God was now using to fuel my passion and the vision He gave me to train, develop, encourage, and mentor youth into a place a purpose and destiny. What I perceived as a problem (my personal situation), God was now using for my personal growth and development. The Bible says in Ephesians 4:26-27 (AMP)

> **"Be angry (at sin-at immorality, at injustice, at ungodly behavior), YET DO NOT SIN; do not let your anger (cause you shame, nor allow it to) last until the sun goes down. And do not give the devil an opportunity (to lead you into sin by holding a grudge, or nurturing anger, or harboring resentment, or cultivating bitterness)."**

Faith To Forgive

"What is perceived as a problem is really a place of personal growth and development."

Anger is a God-given emotion and if used for the right reasons, great things can come out of the emotion of anger. Anger can motivate you to write a book, start a business, create a cure for a terminal disease, or come up with a solution to solve a global crisis like Joseph did with the famine. Joseph was angry about what his brothers did to him, but he did not allow his anger to manifest into bitterness and unforgiveness. Joseph maintained a position of forgiveness and God was able to use him to solve the global economic crisis in his day and time. I was angry about the unfair treatment and onslaught of lies that I had to deal with in my life. Like Joseph, I sought God for wisdom and understanding. As a result, I learned to trust God by faith to protect me and deliver me from my enemies. One of the tricks of satan is to get you to focus your thoughts, speech, and emotional energy on an unjust act that was committed against you. By doing so, you give the devil an opportunity to lead you into sin by nurturing anger, harboring resentment, and or cultivating bitterness in your heart. Satan wants to take what God gave as a gift—in this instance,--"anger"--and manipulate your emotions by magnifying negative experiences in your life. Satan is a tempter and his job is to kill, steal, and destroy (John 10:10). God has a plan for your life, but it cannot come to pass unless you resist the temptations of the devil.

Whatever you don't resist, is allowed to remain!
                                     - Dr. Bill Winston

James 4:7 (AMP) says,

> *"So submit to (the authority of) God. Resist the devil (stand firm against him) and he will flee from you."*

Notice, the first thing that is required is for you to submit to God. Then, you will have the power to stand firm against the devil. As a result, he will now have to flee because of your decision to remain under the authority of God. Your act of faith is to submit to God's word. The word of God will give you the strength to withstand the onslaught of satan's attacks against your mind and your emotions. Faith is the only way to defeat the enemy when he is attacking your mind and trying to manipulate your emotions. This is why the Bible instructs us to put on the full armor of God by faith for protection against the temptations, accusations, and deception of the enemy.

> *"Put on the full armor of God (for His precepts are like the splendid armor of a heavily-armed soldier), so that you may be able to (successfully) stand up against all the schemes and the strategies and the deceits of the devil. For our struggle is not against flesh and blood (contending only with physical opponents), but*

against the rulers, against the powers, against the world forces of this (present) darkness, against the spiritual forces of wickedness in the heavenly (supernatural) places. Therefore, put on the complete armor of God, so that you will be able to (successfully) resist and stand your ground in the evil day (of danger), and having done everything (that the crisis demands), to stand firm (in your place, fully prepared, immovable, victorious). So stand firm and hold your ground, HAVING (personal integrity, moral courage) AROUND YOUR WAIST and HAVING PUT ON THE BREASTPLATE OF RIGHTEOSNESS (an upright heart), and having strapped on YOUR FEET THE GOSPEL OF PEACE IN PREPARATION (to face the enemy with firm-footed stability and the readiness produced by the good news). Above all, lift up the (protective) shield of FAITH with which you can extinguish all the flaming arrows of the evil one. And take THE HELMET OF SALVATION, and the sword of the Spirit, which is the Word of God."

- Ephesians 6:11-17 (AMP)

In my life, the enemy was using personal offenses, false accusations, and emotional hurts to manipulate my feelings. The devil wanted to distract me so that the eyes of my understanding would be blinded to the truth of God's word. If the enemy can manipulate you into a position where you have issues trusting

I Forgive You

God, you can find yourself compromising God's will for your life. If you are not in God's will for your life, you will begin to experience frustration and unfulfillment which leads to a lack of personal value and self-worth. I realized that the plan of God for my life was coming to pass as I began to focus on serving others and took my mind off what I was going through in my personal life. I made a decision to forgive by faith, and as a result, God was able to use me to meet the needs of others and at the same time change the trajectory of my life forever! **It's not about what's happening to you, it's about what God can do through you!**

"…The just shall live by faith!"
– Galatians. 3:11

God expects you and I to live by faith! Everything God promised us in His word was meant to be obtained by faith. By faith, we obtain our healing, our peace, our prosperity, our joy, our safety, our success, and our victory. God expects us to love by faith, to give by faith, to receive by faith, to pray in faith and to forgive by faith! Hebrews 11:6 says,

"But without faith it is impossible to (walk with God and) please Him, for whoever comes (near) to God must (necessarily) believe that God exists and that He rewards those who (earnestly and diligently) seek Him."

__What is FAITH?__

Faith is defined by *American Dictionary of The English Language (Webster's 1828)* as:
"Belief; the assent of the mind to the truth of what is declared by another, resting on his authority and veracity, without other evidence; the judgement that what another states or testifies is the truth; the assent of the mind or understanding to the truth of what God has revealed."

Hebrews 11:1 says,
> *"Now faith is the assurance (title deed, confirmation) of things hoped for (divinely guaranteed), and the evidence of things not seen (the conviction of their reality-faith comprehends as fact what cannot be experienced by the physical senses)."*

Simply stated, faith is believing you have something before you physically have it. You may think it's difficult to live by faith. However, the reality is we live by faith on a daily basis without knowing it. For example, we sit in chairs without a single thought of the chair breaking. I have yet to meet someone who asked me for the weight capacity of a chair before attempting to sit down. When you purchase a new car, the thought never enters into your mind that the engine will not start or the brakes will not work. You have faith in your new purchase therefore, you make travel plans without a concern for car trouble. When we hear the weather forecast for the week, we plan out what we are going to wear based on what we heard. We celebrate and make plans for marriage, parenting, and new employment opportunities (based on information alone--no physical evidence required). This is faith! However, when it comes to managing conflict between people, we typically don't rely on faith because we are so fixated on the moment, the emotions, and the offender! Faith has nothing to do with our five senses: sight, sound, touch, taste, or feel. As a matter-of-fact, if your trust and confidence is based solely on your five senses rather than what God said in His word, you are not in faith at all! Having faith in God means that you absolutely depend on God alone to deliver you out of every negative situation and circumstance. Faith is holding on to what you believe until what you believe is now what you are experiencing in your life. Faith is having the promises of God securely established in your heart before you can actually see it with your natural eyes.

Faith is solely based on what you believe--not what you feel!

When it comes to forgiving others who have hurt us, we tend to put aside our faith because we want to validate our feelings instead of believing God for our deliverance. I warn you, don't be like "Doubting Thomas!" Thomas was one of the twelve disciples who took the position in his heart that unless he saw Jesus and physically touched him with his hands, he

Faith To Forgive

would not allow himself to believe Jesus had risen from the dead.

> *"But Thomas, one of the twelve (disciples), who was called Didymus (the twin), was not with them when Jesus came. So the other disciples kept telling him, "We have seen the Lord!" But he said to them, "Unless I see in His hands the marks of the nails, and put my finger into the nails prints, and put my hand into His side, I will not believe. Eight days later His disciples were again inside the house, and Thomas was with them. Jesus came, though the doors had been barred, and stood among them and said, "Peace to you." Then He said to Thomas, "Reach here with your finger, and see My hands; and put out your hand and place it in My side. Do not be unbelieving, but (stop doubting and) believe." Thomas answered Him, "My Lord and my God!" Jesus said to him, "Because you have seen Me, do you now believe? Blessed (happy, spiritually secure, and favored by God) are they who did not see (Me) and yet believed (in Me)."*
> – John 20:24-29 (AMP)

Thomas needed physical proof that Jesus had risen from the dead in order to believe the reports that Jesus was resurrected. Thomas convinced himself that he needed to see with his own two eyes and physically touch Jesus himself in order to believe. This is how most of us are when it comes to forgiving others. We want visible, tangible, and sustained proof that change has occurred before we would consider forgiving someone who has hurt us. This is what I call the "Doubting Thomas" mentality.

- If I can't see it, I don't believe it!
- If I can't touch it, it didn't happen!

This mentality is the total opposite of faith because faith is believing you have what you desire even when you can't physically touch or see what you are believing for. The "Doubting Thomas" mentality is fear-based. You become more concerned about the opinions of others, rather than your faith in what God said in His word. Jesus said,

"Blessed (happy, spiritually secure, and favored by God) are they who did not see (Me) and yet believed (in Me).
– John 20:29 (AMP).

"So then faith cometh by hearing, and hearing by the word of God
– Romans 10:17 (KJV)

What are you listening to?
Whatever you choose to listen to is what you will develop faith to have! It is very important to understand the power of words and the need to take inventory of what you choose to listen to!

- Are you listening to your feelings?
- Are you listening to your mind?
- Are you listening to your friends and family?
- Are you listening to God?

We live in a society where information is being shared 24/7, 365 days a year! We are constantly bombarded with opinions, philosophies, and doctrines that are rooted in unresolved hurt and unforgiveness. This is why we have to be careful and take inventory of the words we listen to. Faith comes by hearing, and hearing by the word of God! *What are you listening to?*

Faith is like a muscle, the more you work the muscle, the stronger the muscle becomes. The more you listen to the word of faith, the stronger your faith becomes. I attempt to exercise three to four times per week. I understand that a level of consistency in my workouts is required to obtain my fitness goals. Faith works the same way! You have to be consistent in your listening and believing by faith in order to develop your faith. Exercising develops muscle tone, endurance, and strength. Faith develops confidence, assurance, and hope in God's word. When faith is fully developed, your belief becomes stronger in the promise instead of the problem! This is how I was able to move beyond the hurt in my life. I meditated on God's word and His love for me. God's love became my security blanket and I was no longer worried, fearful, ashamed, or embarrassed. God's perfect love drove all the fear out of my heart.

> *"There is no fear in love. But perfect love drives out fear, because fear has to do with punishment. The one who fears is not made perfect in love."*
>
> — 1 John 4:18

-The love of God will drive the fear of satan out of your heart!-

"At one time we too were foolish, disobedient, deceived and enslaved by all kinds of passions and pleasures. We lived in malice and envy, being hated and hating one another. But when the kindness and love of God our Savior appeared, he saved us, not because of righteous things we had done, but because of his mercy. He saved us through the washing rebirth and renewal of the Holy Spirit, whom he poured out on us generously through Jesus Christ our Savior, so that, having been justified by his grace, we might become heirs having the hope of eternal life."

- Titus 3:3-7 (NIV)

Faith To Forgive

God, out of His love, forgave you and I by Faith! You and I out of God's love, must forgive our offenders by Faith!

> *"I am giving you a new commandment, that you love one another. Just as I have loved you, so you too are to love one another. By this everyone will know that you are My disciples, if you have love and unselfish concern for one another."*
>
> - John 13:34-35 (AMP)

You cannot forgive beyond your understanding of God's love. Love activates faith and faith is the key to manifesting victory in your life. If you don't have love, you can't active your faith. If your faith is not activated, you will not have hope. If you don't have hope, you will not obtain the victory. If you don't obtain the victory, you will not have a testimony. Your testimony is the evidence that your faith worked! Your testimony has the power to ignite faith in the hearts of others to believe God for breakthrough in their lives! Satan wants to use unforgiveness to steal your testimony. The devil understands that your testimony is the proof that your faith works, and God's word is true. Your testimony is the proof that what God promised you in His word came to pass in your life. Your testimony is proof that satan is a liar! Your testimony is what God use to encourage, energize, and motivate others to live by faith. The devil wants to kill, steal, and destroy your testimony. Your testimony validates God's word and ignites faith to overcome the works of the devil.

> *"And they overcame and conquered him because of the blood of the Lamb and because of the word of their testimony..."*
>
> – Rev. 12:11 (AMP)

Your testimony validates God's word and ignites faith to overcome the devil!

Speak the Word!

God is love and full of mercy! God wants to see you delivered from the root of bitterness, resentment, and unforgiveness. God has given His word for you and I to speak over our situations in order to obtain victory in our lives. Proverbs 18:21 says,

> **"That life and death is in the power of the tongue."**

When we speak God's word in faith, we release God's power into our lives to deliver us from every attack of the enemy. God has given you faith to forgive! Forgiveness is about you and your relationship with Christ. Forgiveness is a decision and an attitude that says, "it does not matter what you did, **I Forgive You!**

Faith To Forgive

Repeat this prayer by Faith:

Father, I come to You in the Mighty Name of Jesus asking for faith to forgive. You said in Your Word in Romans 1:17, "The righteous will live by faith." You said in Mark 11:24, "Therefore I tell you, whatever you ask for in prayer, believe that you have received it, and it will be yours." You said in John 14:14, "If I ask You anything in Your name, You will do it!" Therefore, in the name of Jesus, I ask that You purge my heart from the root of bitterness, offense, and hurt. Fill my heart with Your love, peace, and joy. Give me faith to forgive in Jesus' Name.

Amen!

Chapter IV: Faith to Forgive!

<u>Key Principles</u>

- ❏ **Forgiveness is not a sign of weakness-it requires strength!**
- ❏ **What is perceived as a problem is really a place of personal growth and development**
- ❏ **Jesus forgave you by faith!**
- ❏ **Faith is solely based on what you believe, not what you feel!**
- ❏ **God expects you to live, love, and forgive by faith!**
- ❏ **Love activates faith!**
- ❏ **Faith comes by hearing the Word of God!**
- ❏ **Your testimony ignites faith in others to believe God!**
- ❏ **It's not about what happened to you, it's about what God can do through you!**
- ❏ **Speak the Word!**

<u>Meditation Scriptures</u>

Luke 17:3-5 (NIV)
"If your brother or sister sins against you, rebuke them; and if they repent, forgive them. Even if they sin against you seven times in a day and seven times come back to you saying 'I repent,' you must forgive

Faith To Forgive

them." The apostles said to the Lord, "Increase our faith!"

Luke 11:4 **(MSG)**
"Keep us forgiven with you and forgiving others."

Ephesians 4:26-27 (AMP)
"Be angry (at sin-at immorality, at injustice, at ungodly behavior), YET DO NOT SIN; do not let your anger (cause you shame, nor allow it to) last until the sun goes down. And do not give the devil an opportunity (to lead you into sin by holding a grudge, or nurturing anger, or harboring resentment, or cultivating bitterness)."

Hebrews 11:6 (AMP)
"But without faith it is impossible to (walk with God and) please Him, for whoever comes (near) to God must (necessarily) believe that God exists and that He rewards those who (earnestly and diligently) seek Him."

Hebrews 11:1 (AMP)
"Now faith is the assurance (title deed, confirmation) of things hoped for (divinely guaranteed), and the evidence of things not seen (the conviction of their reality-faith comprehends as fact what cannot be experienced by the physical senses)."

Chapter VI: Reflection Questions

The writer says "Forgiveness is not a position of the weak--it's a position of the strong!" What does this mean to you? In your opinion, why is strength an important element in the forgiving process?

_____
_____
_____
_____
_____
_____
_____
_____
_____
_____

The writer talks about Faith to Forgive. In your opinion, what is faith? Why is faith an important factor in the forgiving process?

_____
_____
_____
_____
_____
_____

Faith To Forgive

_____
_____
_____
_____

"What is perceived as a problem is really a place of personal growth and development." What does this mean to you? How can you utilize this perspective to remain encouraged when your faith is weak?

_____
_____
_____
_____
_____
_____
_____
_____
_____
_____
_____

Do you have a "Doubting Thomas" mentality when it comes to forgiving others? Explain

_____
_____
_____
_____

I Forgive You

_____
_____

As you reflect on the chapter and some of the personal information that the author shared about his life experiences, ask yourself the following questions:

- **What?**
- **So, what?**
- **Now, what?**

Begin with defining and sharing **"what"** facts and events the author shared in the chapter, *Faith To Forgive*.

"So, what" did you learn about yourself as a result of what the author shared?

"Now, what" learning occurred for you as a result of this shared experience? How will you apply what you learned in order to help you appropriately respond when offended?
Use the reflection notes to respond.

Personal Reflection Notes:

_____
_____
_____
_____
_____
_____

Faith To Forgive

I Forgive You

Chapter V
The Key to Freedom

"Be kind and helpful to one another, tender-hearted (compassionate, understanding) forgiving one another (readily and freely), just as God in Christ also forgave you."
– Ephesians 4:32 (AMP)

"It's not an easy journey, to get to a place where you forgive people. But it is such a powerful place, because it frees you."
-Tyler Perry, American, Self-made millionaire, actor, comedian, producer, and filmmaker

The journey to forgive can be a hard and lonely process. It is not an easy journey; however, the final destination—freedom—is a powerful location once you arrive. Everyone at some point in their lives has had to deal with the emotions of rejection, disappointment, bitterness, betrayal, broken promises,

I Forgive You

offense, and unforgiveness. I have learned personally that when offense came, the lasting impact of that offense was determined by my attitude. After the death of my parents, I developed a negative attitude about my life, my future, and my day to day decisions. I lost my motivation and determination to succeed. I dwelt in the place of despair and hopelessness for a long time. I justified the feelings of bitterness and unforgiveness with the mindset that I had a bad lease on life. I was angry and I felt enslaved to my emotions. No matter how much I smiled and pretended to be okay, the emotional pain and emptiness continued to grow deeper and deeper in my heart. What I did not realize was the longer the unforgiveness remained in my heart, the deeper the toxicity became in other areas of my life.

"The longer you wait to forgive, the deeper the toxicity becomes in your life!"

For years, I harbored unforgiveness and resentment towards my parents after their deaths. All bitterness doesn't just come by what happened. Sometimes, bitterness comes into your life based on what did not happen. I developed a deeper grudge towards my father because he did not make a decision to stop drinking alcohol even after his doctors advised him to quit. He continued to drink which was the primary cause of his debilitating health which ultimately lead to his early death. The unforgiveness in my heart was not only defiling my relationships, it was defiling my

The Key to Freedom

health. Unforgiveness is very toxic and dangerous. If you allow unforgiveness to remain in your life, it will eventually manifest into physical sickness in your body. There are countless medical studies that show the direct correlation between sickness and unforgiveness. In an article entitled: "The Deadly Consequences of Unforgiveness," published June 22, 2015, CBN.com, (Johnson, L. 2015, June 22, The Deadly Consequences of Unforgiveness. Retrieved from http://CBN.com), the article states, "Unforgiveness is classified in medical books as a disease and refusing to forgive makes people sick and keeps them that way." The article goes on to say that "Of all cancer patients, 61 percent have forgiveness issues." "Harboring these negative emotions creates a state of chronic anxiety." "Chronic anxiety very predictably produces excess adrenaline and cortisol, which deplete the production of natural killer cells, which is your body's foot soldier in the fight against cancer." It has also been stated that unforgiveness is linked to other medical conditions such as arthritis, high blood pressure, various forms of depression and mental illness. Unforgiveness will not only enslave you, it will destroy your relationships and ultimately kill you!

I Forgive You

"Hate is self-destructive. If you hate somebody, you're not hurting the person you hate. You're hurting yourself. And that's a healing. Actually, it's a real healing, forgiveness."
-Louis Zamperini, World War II hero and Olympian whose life the number one New York best seller "Unbroken" was based upon

UNRESOLVED UNFORGIVENESS IS SELF-DESTRUCTIVE!

> **"Blessed and happy and favored are those whose lawless acts have been forgiven, and whose sins have been covered up and completely buried!"**
>
> - Romans 4:7 (AMP)

The feelings of hurt, rejection, and resentment tormented me throughout my teenage years into my young adult life. It wasn't until I heard the message of God's love, grace, and mercy one Sunday morning while attending University Baptist Church on Eastern Illinois University's campus. Listening to the pastor articulate the message seemed as if the pastor had watched my entire life play out. The message that the pastor preached spoke directly to the hurt, abandonment, and rejection I felt as a child through my early adult years. The message revealed to me God's love, His grace, the power of Jesus's blood that cleansed me, and the finished work of Jesus Christ on Calvary that separates me from my sin and my past! I was finally free from the bondage of my past! I realized that letting go of my past wasn't just about letting go of what happened… it was about letting go of what didn't happen. I was bitter because I didn't have the experience of growing up with my parents. I had to let go of what didn't happen so that I could embrace what could now happen in my life. Over time, God began to mend the brokenness in my life, heal my emotional hurts, and reveal to me that I was good, useful, special, and that my life had purpose and value. God began to show me that He had thoughts of peace and not of evil towards me, and that He would give me hope for a brighter future.

> **"For I know the plans and thoughts that I have for you, says the Lord, plans for peace and well-being and not for disaster to give you a future and a hope."**
> – Jeremiah 29:11 (AMP)

The Lord began to show me that in order for me to manifest His peace in my life, I needed to forgive and release anyone who had hurt me. I needed to forgive my parents for abandoning me. I needed to forgive friends who betrayed my trust. I needed to forgive myself so I could embrace the future God promised me in His word. At that moment, I realized forgiveness was indeed for me!

Forgiveness Is for You!

I Forgive You

You may feel like you can't get over what was said to you! You may feel like you can't get over what was done to you! Your intentions were good and your motives were pure. However, things may have happened in your life and as a result you are stuck in that place of hurt and disappointment from a relationship that ended some ten, fifteen, or twenty years ago. Regardless of the hurt or injustice you have been subjected to, you've now allowed satan an entry point into your life. Now he has access to your mind and wreaks havoc as he replays the episodes of hurt over and over and over again.

God wants you free from all toxic waste in your life! God wants you free to love, free to be creative, free to live a good life, and free to fulfill your destiny. I urge you to forgive that person who hurt you! Forgive that friend who betrayed your trust! Forgive that spouse who was unfaithful to you! Forgive that parent who let you down! Forgive that boss who overlooked you for that promotion! Forgive that child who disappointed you! Forgive yourself! When you forgive it doesn't free the offender, forgiveness liberates you! Forgiveness is a gift to yourself!

Forgiveness is about empowering yourself, rather than empowering your past.
- T. D. Jakes

The Key to Freedom

- Forgiveness is for your sake!
- Forgiveness liberates you!
- Forgiveness is a gift to yourself!
- Forgiveness empowers you!

When you forgive, you unclog your heart. This in turn allows God to flow into your life and move you past the feelings of hurt, resentment, disappointment, and bitterness. When you forgive, the deadly poisons and toxins that the devil tries to use to destroy your health and steal your joy are now being flushed from your heart so that you can be free! When you forgive, you separate yourself from your past and you position yourself to embrace the future and the hope God has for you. When you forgive, you say "Yes" to God and "No" to the devil. However, you cannot and will not move forward in your life until you make the decision to forgive. The enemy's strategy is simple, he wants you to hold on to grudges and unforgiveness so that God will not exempt you from your sin! The Bible says when you refuse to forgive others, the wages of your sin that were pardoned will now require full payment! The parable of the unmerciful servant is an excellent example of the benefit and importance of forgiving others.

> **"Therefore, the kingdom of heaven is like a king who wanted to settle accounts with his servants. As he began the settlement, a man who owed him ten thousand bags of gold was brought to him. Since he was not able to pay,**

I Forgive You

the master ordered that he and his wife and his children and all that he had be sold to repay the debt. At this the servant fell on his knees before him. 'Be patient with me,' he begged, 'and I will pay back everything.' The servant's master took pity on him, canceled the debt and let him go. "But when that servant went out, he found one of his fellow servants who owed him a hundred silver coins. He grabbed him and began to choke him. 'Pay back what you owe me!' he demanded. "His fellow servant fell to his knees and begged him, 'Be patient with me, and I will pay it back.' "But he refused. Instead, he went off and had the man thrown into prison until he could pay the debt. When the other servants saw what happened, they were outraged and went and told their master everything that had happened. "Then the master called the servant in. 'You wicked servant,' he said, 'I canceled all that debt of yours because you begged me to. Shouldn't you have had mercy on your fellow servant just as I had on you?' In anger, his master handed him over to the jailers to be tortured, until he should pay back all he owed. "This is how my heavenly Father will treat each of you unless you forgive your brother or sister from your heart."

- Matthew 18:23-35 (NIV)

FORGIVENESS IS THE KEY TO FREEDOM!

I once heard a story about a man who was sentenced to prison for thirty years for a murder he didn't commit. The man said every day for the first ten years of his imprisonment, all he thought about day and night was how he would take revenge against the person who lied on him. He swore to himself that if he ever saw the man that lied on him he would kill him. He maintained this position of hatred, bitterness, and unforgiveness for years until one day he heard a preacher share God's redemptive message of love, peace, and restoration. After hearing the message of hope, he opened his heart to Jesus and invited Him into his life to be his personal Lord and Savior. The Lord began to deal with his heart and regulate his thoughts. He began to read the Bible daily. One day he was lead to read Matthew 6:14-15,

"For if you forgive others their trespasses (their reckless and willful sins), your heavenly Father will also forgive you. But if you do not forgive others (nurturing your hurt and anger with the result that it interferes with your relationship with God), then your Father will not forgive your trespasses." (AMP)

In that moment, he realized that he needed God's grace, love, mercy, and forgiveness. Therefore, he had to extend grace, love, mercy, and forgiveness to his accuser. The Bible says in Luke 6:37-38,

> **"Do not judge, and you will not be judged. Do not condemn, and you will not be condemned. Forgive, and you will be forgiven. Give, and it will be given to you."** (NIV)

He made the decision that day to forgive his accuser by faith and to trust God to teach him how to turn the other cheek. The feelings of hatred and revenge that once overwhelmed his heart towards his accuser were now being replaced with feelings of love and compassion. The hope he obtained from God's word gave him a sense of freedom beyond the walls of containment.

> **"So if the Son makes you free, then you are unquestionably free."**
> - John 8:36 (AMP)

The man who was incarcerated was finally free from the bondage of bitterness, resentfulness, and unforgiveness. He was free to love, forgive, and now bless his enemies. The gentleman who lied and had the guy arrested was living a life of daily torment. He knew he was wrong and as a result, an innocent man was now serving thirty years of his life behind bars for a crime he did not commit. This man was struggling with the guilt and shame of what he had done. He eventually could not take it any longer and decided to come forward with the truth. The man who was falsely accused was finally freed of all charges. He was totally exonerated!

The Key to Freedom

The gentleman who lied, had a strong desire to meet face-to-face with the man he falsely accused of murder. He felt in his heart that coming forth with the truth was only part of the reconciliation process. The second part of the process for him was to apologize for his actions. He felt the need to ask for forgiveness for his actions and the hurt inflicted as a result of lies he told. Initially, the man who was accused of murder did not want to meet. In his mind, there was no reason for a face-to-face meeting. However, after he prayed about it, he felt the Lord leading him to move forward with the face-to-face meeting. He decided to meet and the arrangements were made.

When they finally met, the innocent man who was falsely accused had a countenance of peace, joy, and comfort. He outwardly displayed God's love and embraced his accuser. On the other hand, the man who lied had a very nervous, sad, and despondent countenance. His face was awash with regret, shame and hopelessness. He began to speak the following words, "I've been tormented for years and I've had absolutely no peace since falsely accusing you of something you did not do." He went on the say with tears running down his is face, "I am so sorry for what I did to you! Will you please forgive me? I need you to forgive me!" The man who was falsely accused, replied, "My brother, I forgave you a long time ago! I had to forgive you because every minute, hour, and day I spent behind bars was a constant

I Forgive You

reminder of the lies that were told and my anger eventually grew into rage. I wanted to take revenge! Every day all I could think about was hurting you for what you did to me. However, I realized that what was done was done! Even though I was physically locked behind bars, I refused to be a prisoner emotionally, mentally, and spiritually. Therefore, I made a decision to move on with my life. I had to break free and the only way I was able to break away from the bondage of unforgiveness was to forgive you! Once I received Christ into my heart, I understood that I was forgiven and in order to be forgiven, I had a responsibility as a Christian to forgive! I learned through God's word that I could forgive by faith. In order for me to move forward in my life, I had to forgive! Therefore, I say as we stand eye-to-eye, I forgive you! The man who lied began to weep uncontrollably and spoke the following words, even though I was physically free, I was mentally, emotionally, and spiritually imprisoned with the guilt and shame of what I did to you. I needed to hear you say that you forgive me, so that I could forgive myself! Thank you for freeing me—now I can be free!

"Forgiveness is for yourself because it frees you. It lets you out of that prison you put yourself in."
- Louise L. Hay, American motivational author and founder of the Hay House

The Key to Freedom

This story is so powerful because it shows the mental, emotional, and spiritual bondage of unforgiveness. It also shows the power and freedom that comes through forgiveness because forgiveness liberates you. It is a gift that you give yourself!

FORGIVENESS IS A GIFT THAT YOU GIVE YOURSELF!

Both men needed to be liberated! The man that lied needed to forgive himself. The man who was falsely accused needed to forgive his accuser. Deliverance is needed for both the oppressed and the oppressor! You can be physically free but mentally, emotionally, and spiritually incarcerated. I realized that every time I was hurt, disappointed, falsely accused, misused, and set up to fail; and if I wanted to move forward with my life, I had to forgive no matter how deep the pain and disappointment. Forgiveness is not an easy journey. However, it is a powerful destination because it frees you from your past!

FORGIVENESS RELEASES YOU FROM YOUR PAST AND POSITIONS YOU TO EMBRACE YOUR FUTURE!

Take for example the ministry of the Apostle Paul. Before Paul began his ministry that credits him for writing over half the New Testament in the Bible, he was formerly known as Saul. The Apostle Paul received God's grace, mercy, and forgiveness for

I Forgive You

years of terrorizing Christians because they proclaimed the Gospel of Jesus Christ. Saul was a modern-day terrorist! After Saul, accepted Christ into his heart, he began a new journey in his life as the Apostle Paul preaching and proclaiming to the world the gospel of Jesus Christ with signs and wonders confirming the word preached! The power of God's love and his forgiveness released Saul from his horrific past and gave Paul a hope to embrace his future.

> **"Therefore there is now no condemnation (no guilt verdict, no punishment) for those who are in Christ Jesus (who believe in Him as personal Lord and Savior). For the law of the Spirit of life (which is) in Christ Jesus (the law of our new being) has set you free from the law of sin and death. For what the Law could not do (that is, overcome sin and remove its penalty, its power) being weakened by the flesh (man's nature without the Holy Spirit), God did: He sent His own Son in the likeness of sinful man as an offering for sin. And He condemned sin in the flesh (subdued it and overcame it in the person of His own Son), so that the (righteous and just) requirement of the Law might be fulfilled in us who do not live our lives in the way of the flesh (guided by worldliness and our sinful nature), but (live our lives) in the ways of the Spirit (guided by His power)."**
> — Romans 8:1-4 (AMP)

The Key to Freedom

-God's forgiveness releases you from the guilt and shame of your past!-

Forgiveness releases you from the guilt and shame of your past. The Apostle Paul walked in God's grace, mercy, love, and forgiveness. The book of Acts chapters 9 through 28 gives a clear illustration of the transformational process in the life of Paul.

From Saul to the Apostle Paul

Saul	Paul
Persecutor	Encourager
Murderer	Friend / Ally
Killed to stop the Gospel	Died to Spread the Gospel
Servant to Satan	Servant to Jesus
Self-Conscience	God-Conscience
Bound By Religion	Freedom in Christ
Fear-based Ministry	Faith-Based Ministry
Legacy of Death	Legacy of Life

I Forgive You

"If we (freely) admit that we have sinned and confess our sins, He is faithful and just (true to His own nature and promises), and will forgive our sins and cleanse us continually from all unrighteousness (our wrongdoing, everything not in conformity with His will and purpose).
- 1 John 1:9 (AMP)

The Apostle Paul understood that God loved him and had a plan and purpose for his life. Paul confessed his sins and wrongdoings before God so that he could be cleansed continually from all unrighteousness and everything not in conformity with God's will for his life. The only sin that is unforgiven is the sin that is not confessed! Paul understood that in order for him to fulfill his calling and assignment he needed to be cleansed from his horrific past.

- What sin do you need forgiven in your life?
- What wrongdoings do you need to confess before God?

According to 1 John 1:9, confess and believe you have received by faith, God's forgiveness from all unrighteousness (wrongdoing, everything not in conformity to God's will and purpose) for your life.

The Key to Freedom

~ Forgiveness releases God's will and purpose for your life ~

The story of Joseph is a true testament of the fact that there is greatness in your life that is released through the pain that you suffer. Joseph refused to allow offense and unforgiveness to hinder or stop the conformity of God's will and purpose from coming to pass in his life. Instead of Joseph's brothers looking at the mission/assignment God placed on the inside of Joseph, they focused on the position God placed him in over them and this caused them to hate their brother rather than embracing their brother. Sometimes people can't celebrate your position in life because they don't understand your mission in life! The world and the religious leaders did not understand Jesus's mission and this is why they wanted to kill him. Yet, when he was dying on the cross, he began to intercede for his accusers and prayed the most powerful prayer ever prayed in Luke 23:34. Jesus recognized that forgiveness was the will of God. Therefore, before he died, he not only released his accusers, he maintained the integrity of his assignment.

> **"Father, forgive them, for they do not know what they are doing!"**
>
> - Luke 23:34 (AMP)

YOUR POSITION IN LIFE SPEAKS TO YOUR MISSION IN LIFE!

I Forgive You

The extreme pressure that Joseph faced in his life was designed to move him into an offensive position of unforgiveness. Joseph was rejected by his family, sold into slavery, falsely accused, imprisoned, and betrayed. Yet Joseph, like Jesus, did not allow unforgiveness to clog up his heart and stop the will of God in his life. Joseph understood that forgiveness was the key to manifest God's will and purpose in his life.

> **"Then Joseph could not control himself (any longer) in front of all those who attended him, and he called out, "Have everyone leave me." So no man stood there when Joseph revealed himself to his brothers. Joseph wept aloud, and the Egyptians (who had just left him) heard it, and the household of Pharaoh heard of it. Then Joseph said to his brothers, "I am Joseph! Is my father still alive?" But his brothers were speechless, for they were stunned and dismayed by (the fact that they were in) Joseph's presence. And Joseph said to his brothers, "Please come closer to me." And they approached him. And he said, "I am Joseph your brother, whom you sold into Egypt. Now do not be distressed or angry with yourselves because you sold me here, for God sent me ahead of you to save life and preserve our family. For the famine has been in the land these two years, and there is still five more**

The Key to Freedom

years in which there will be no plowing and harvesting. God sent me (to Egypt) ahead of you to preserve for you a remnant on the earth, and to keep you alive by a great escape. So now it was not you who sent me here, but God; and He has made me a father to Pharaoh and lord of all his household and ruler over all the land of Egypt.

- Genesis 45:1-8 (AMP)

"There is greatness in your pain!"

The greatness in Joseph's life came forth because God allowed Joseph to endure heartbreak, separation anxiety, emotional trauma, disappointment, betrayal, false accusations, and rejection. Joseph's personal hardships built character, emotional strength, faith, and integrity. As a result of Joseph consistently overcoming offense, trusting God, and not allowing unforgiveness to set up in his heart, Joseph was elevated to be second in command over all of Egypt. Instead of Joseph retaliating against his brothers, he ministered grace and comfort to them. Joseph let go of the pain, resentment, and hurt because he understood that what his brothers intended for his demise, God turned for his good. God used the pain and persecution that Joseph endured to orchestrate Joseph's steps and to bring forth growth, purpose, and elevation in Joseph's life.

I Forgive You

The dream that God gave Joseph where he was standing above his brothers and they were kneeling before him finally came to pass! Joseph made a decision to focus on his mission (assignment) and not allow the bad experiences in his life to taint his heart. As a result, Joseph was able to be a blessing to the very people who mistreated him in the first place - his family. Joseph maintained a heart that was pure before God and this kept him from sinking into the sea of unforgiveness. Be careful how you treat people because the very person you are mistreating could have the answer to your problem. Remember, what you sow you will reap!

Joseph was the man God appointed to stand in the gap on behalf of his family and to offer a solution to the famine. The devil came after Jesus and Joseph just like he comes after you and me to bring offense, bitterness, strife, anger, and unforgiveness. The enemy knows the boundaries of your life are in your heart, so he wants to contaminate your heart to remove you from the will of God, because forgiveness is the will of God!

> **"I looked for someone among them who would build up the wall and stand before me in the gap on behalf of the land so I would not have to destroy it…"**
>
> – Ezekiel 22:30 (NIV)

The Key to Freedom

What will be your story?
- How will your life impact the world?
- What mark will you leave behind?
- Will you allow unforgiveness to stop the plan of God in your life?
- Will you be the next Paul or will you be the next Judas?

Forgiveness Empowers You to Fulfill the Mission God Has for Your Life!

Paul and Judas had personal encounters with Jesus. Both Paul and Judas witnessed God's miracle working power and heard countless testimonies about the works of Jesus. The difference between the two was that Paul received God's grace and as a result, he walked in the power of forgiveness. Paul successfully fulfilled the mission that God placed on the inside of him and as a result, we can read about Paul's journey and receive the same message of grace and forgiveness! Judas, on the other hand, rejected God's love and forgiveness and he allowed shame, disgrace, betrayal, condemnation, failure, and guilt to lead him to commit suicide. Will you allow forgiveness to free you like Paul, or will you allow unforgiveness to enslave you like Judas and compromise God's will for your life?

I Forgive You

"It's important to recognize that forgiveness is more than mere words; it's a heart attitude that induces a spiritual transformation."
 - Victoria Osteen, <u>is the co-pastor of Lakewood Church in Houston, Texas, an author, the wife of Joel Osteen, an American televangelist</u>

Forgiveness is a matter of the HEART!

Forgiveness is more than mere words, it's a matter of the heart! If what's in your heart is right then, what will come out of your heart will be right! The story of "The Lost Son" is a great example of the father having the right "heart attitude" towards his son even when his son rebelled against his wishes. The father's "heart attitude" was one of love, compassion, and forgiveness for his son.

> **"There was a man who had two sons. The younger one said to his father, 'Father, give me my share of the estate.' So he divided his property between them. "Not long after that, the younger son got together all he had, set off for a distant country and there squandered his wealth on wild living. After he had spent everything, there was a severe famine in that whole country, and he began to be in need. So he went and hired himself out to a citizen of that country, who sent him to his fields to feed pigs. He longed to fill his stomach with the pods that the pigs were eating, but no one gave**

The Key to Freedom

him anything. "When he came to his senses, he said, 'How many of my father's hired servants have food to spare, and here I am starving to death! I will set out and go back to my father and say to him: Father, I have sinned against heaven and against you. I am no longer worthy to be called your son; make me like one of your hired servants.' So he got up and went to his father. "But while he was still a long way off, his father saw him and was filled with compassion for him; he ran to his son, threw his arms around him and kissed him. "The son said to him, 'Father, I have sinned against heaven and against you. I am no longer worthy to be called your son.' "But the father said to his servants, 'Quick! Bring the best robe and put it on him. Put a ring on his finger and sandals on his feet. Bring the fattened calf and kill it. Let's have a feast and celebrate. For this son of mine was dead and is alive again; he was lost and is found.' So they began to celebrate."

- Luke 15:12-24 (NIV)

This story is so dear and near to me because I am a father, and I have sons. The primary character in this story is the lost son. The parable speaks about the condition of his heart and the consequences of his choices. The parable doesn't say much about the unsung hero in my opinion who happens to be the father. The reason why this story has such profound

I Forgive You

meaning to me is because the end of the story would not have happened if the father did not forgive his son in the beginning. I'm sure like most parents, the father in the story had high expectations for his son. I'm sure the father wanted his son to have a better life then himself. I'm sure the father wanted his son to adhere to his wisdom and follow his example of success. I'm sure the father did not want his son to waste his inheritance, but to invest it wisely. However, like most kids, the lost son decided that he didn't need his father's example, his words of wisdom, or his support any longer. He decided that he was old enough to make his own decisions and he could finally do things his way! The father had to have the right "heart attitude" to forgive his son for his rebellious ways so that he could maintain a position of prayer and intercession on behalf of his son until "he came to his senses." What makes this story so special is that it speaks to the power of humility that leads to forgiveness. This story gives a powerful example of how perfect love can restore a broken relationship between a parent and a child. To any parent that reads this book, I encourage you to maintain the right "heart attitude" towards your children no matter what they do. Make the decision in your mind and store up forgiveness in your heart before your children disappoint you, rebel against you, lie to you, disrespect you, or dishonor you. I have personally experienced hurt and extreme disappointment as a result of the actions of my own children. However, like the father in "The Parable of

The Key to Freedom

the Lost Son," I had to keep vigilant watch and guard over my heart so that my anger would not turn into unforgiveness towards my children. Instead of rehearsing the disappointments, my wife and I would consistently pray and speak the word of God over our children. We would pray for restored relationships, redeemed time, new opportunities to show love towards our children even in the mist of dealing with the hurt and disappointment of their actions. We as parents have to maintain the right "heart attitude" that will foster an environment where God's anointing is present to remove every burden and destroy every yoke. Satan is out to kill, steal, and destroy our children. I encourage you to forgive your children and ask for their forgiveness if you inflicted hurt and disappointment in their lives. We have to set an atmosphere that is filled with love so when our children "come to their senses," we as parents can celebrate their return and restore them to their rightful place like the father did in "The Parable of The Lost Son."

"Keep vigilant watch over your heart; that's where life starts."
- Proverbs 4:23 (MSG)

It's imperative to keep vigilant watch over your heart to guard against situations and personal experiences that have the capacity to breed unforgiveness. Unforgiveness is like carbon monoxide. It's colorless and odorless yet, extremely dangerous! If undetected,

I Forgive You

unforgiveness, like carbon monoxide can be fatal! The same safety precautions we take to guard our homes against carbon monoxide poisoning is how we should guard our hearts against the poison of unforgiveness. Guard your heart from negative people. Guard your heart from people who attempt to hurt you. God wants you free from hurt and pain. God wants you free from rejection and shame. God wants you free from abandonment and disappointment. God wants you free from failure, bitterness, and unforgiveness, so that you can move forward with your life. God wants you to forgive so that you can take back your power and walk into your God-ordained destiny. Forgiveness is not a feeling, it's a decision.

"Keep Us Forgiven with You and Forgiving Others."

- Luke 11:2 (MSG)

How do you uproot the seed of unforgiveness and take back your power?

The very first thing you need to understand in the process of forgiving, is that forgiveness is not a feeling, it's a decision! Repeat after me, **"Forgiveness is not a feeling, it's a decision!"** The main reason people struggle with forgiving is because they haven't made a decision to forgive! If you follow your emotions, you will never forgive because your feelings are real. If you are not watchful and careful, satan will manipulate your feelings and hijack your thought life until you are drowning in the sea of unforgiveness. I recommend that you meditate, rehearse, and memorize these steps to manifest forgiveness in your life.

First Things First!

- Understand, forgiveness is not a feeling, it's a decision.
- Understand, forgiveness is about you, and not the other person(s).
- Understand, forgiving gives you back your power.
- Understand, forgiving breaks the burden and removes the yoke of offense in your life.

Faith is The Prerequisite to Forgive:

You are on a journey of learning, becoming, changing, growing and maturing daily. Everything is a process and the Bible says in Romans 1:17

"The just shall live by faith..."

God wants to channel good things in and through your life but the only way to receive anything from God is by faith. If you allow your heart, soul, mind, will, and emotions to be clogged with bitterness and unforgiveness, your heart becomes tainted, your love-walk compromised, and faith will not work in your life. It takes faith to manifest the fruit of the Spirit which gives you the power to forgive

> **"But the fruit of the Spirit (the result of His presence within us) is love (unselfish concern for others), joy (inner) peace, patience (not the ability to wait, but how we act while waiting), kindness, goodness, faithfulness, gentleness, self-control."**
> - Gal. 5:22-23 (AMP)

> **"So submit to (the authority of) God. Resist the devil (stand firm against him) and he will flee from you."**
> – James 4:7 (AMP)

Before the process of forgiveness can take place in your life, you have to make a conscious decision to submit to the authority of God. Come hell or high water, you have to believe by faith according to Psalms 34:19,

> **"Many hardships and perplexing circumstances confront the righteous, But the Lord rescues him from them all."**

Remember what Victoria Osteen said, **"It's important to recognize that forgiveness is more than mere words; it's a heart attitude that induces a spiritual transformation."** So, in order to experience this spiritual transformation in our lives, we have to understand that forgiveness goes beyond mere words. We have to submit heart, soul, mind, will, and emotions to the authority of God. Then, and only then, can we resist the devil and stand firm against him. Our submission to God takes away the power of the enemy to control and manipulate our emotions because we are now forgiving by FAITH, not by how we FEEL! Therefore, the devil has no choice but to flee because your decision to forgive gives you back the POWER!

The 3 Step Process to Manifest Forgiveness in Your Life:

1. ***Make the decision to forgive by faith.*** Your decision to forgive by faith will uproot the emotions of bitterness and start the healing process which is not based on feelings but your decision. **"The righteous will live by faith."** Romans 1:17 (NIV)

2. ***Resist the temptation to act out of your emotions.*** You will have constant reminders of the hurt, rejections, and emotional pain you experienced in your life. However, your decision to forgive by faith gives you authority over your emotions. So, instead of you acting out of your emotions and your feelings, you will begin to act by faith and your submission to God will compel you to do the following:

I Forgive You

"But I say to you who hear (Me and pay attention to My words): Love (that is, unselfishly seek the best or higher good for) your enemies, (make it a practice to) do good to those who hate you, bless and show kindness to those who curse you, pray for those who mistreat you. Whoever strikes you on the cheek, offer him the other one also (simply ignore insignificant insults or losses and do not bother to retaliate – maintain your dignity). Whoever takes away your coat, do not withhold your shirt from him either."
- Luke 6:27-30 (AMP)

"But love (that is, unselfishly seek the best or higher good for) your enemies, and do good, and lend, expecting nothing in return; for your reward will be great (rich, abundant), and you will be sons of the Most High; because He Himself is kind and gracious and good to the ungrateful and the wicked. Be merciful (responsive, compassionate, tender) just as your (heavenly) Father is merciful."
-Luke 6:35-36 (AMP)

3. *<u>Take control over negative thoughts by speaking positive words about your situation, circumstance, or offender.</u>* You have to take control over your feelings or your feelings are going to control you! You

have to consistently resist the urge to follow the negative thoughts and feelings when the enemy reminds you of your past hurts and disappointments. Your decision to "RESIST" negative thoughts and feelings will bring these feelings captive to your positive confessions. In my profession as a mental health therapist, we call this process "cognitive restructuring" which is a psychotherapeutic process of learning to identify and dispute irrational or maladaptive thought patterns. The Christian community calls this process "renewing the mind" which is a process of meditating and speaking God's promises until that promise is real in your heart, and subsequently manifested and produced in your life.

"This Book of the Law shall not depart from your mouth, but you shall read (and meditate on) it day and night, so that you may be careful to do (everything) in accordance with all that is written in it; for then you will make your way prosperous, and then you will be successful."
- Joshua 1:8 (AMP)

When you meditate and feed your faith with God's word according to Joshua 1:8, your faith will begin to get stronger and stronger until your faith eventually becomes the driver of your decision-making process. Meditating God's word will build your capacity to receive what the word of God says you can have in your life. When you meditate on God's word, you are denying your feelings and replacing negative thoughts with positive thoughts. The more you think about positive outcomes the less time and energy you will give to the negative thoughts and feelings. Over time, the negative feelings and thoughts become weaker and weaker until your new responses will not be:

- ✓ TURN THE OTHER CHEEK!
- ✓ FORGIVE YOUR ENEMIES!
- ✓ PRAY FOR GOOD THINGS TO HAPPENED TO THE PERSON WHO WRONGED YOU!
- ✓ KEEP DOING GOOD NO MATTER WHAT!

THE WAITING PROCESS!

"But if we hope for what we do not see, we wait eagerly for it with patience and composure."
– Romans 8:25 (AMP)

Forgiveness is not an easy process but with God all things become possible! Faith like everything else is developed over time. When someone offends you, it's not easy to wipe away the feelings like you would wipe water off your car. This is not some magic trick or snapping of the fingers or clicking of your heels and now all the hurt is gone! It takes time. However, like it's written in Romans 8:25,

"But if we hope for what we do not see, we wait eagerly for it with patience and composure."

> **"By your (patient) endurance (empowered by the Holy Spirit) you will gain your souls."**
> - Luke 21:19 (AMP)

Remember your soul consists of your mind, will, and emotions. So, when the scripture speaks about you gaining your soul, this is a direct result of denying your feelings to control and dictate your responses. Instead, through patience and endurance, over time you reap the reward by allowing God's word to control and dictate your responses to offense. Your reward is your protection and your deliverance!

> **"Let us not grow weary or become discouraged in doing good, for at the proper time we will reap, if we do not give in. So then, while we (as individual believers) have the opportunity, let us do good to all people (not only being helpful, but also doing that which promotes their spiritual well-being), and especially (be a blessing) to those of the house of faith (born-again believers). "**
> – Galatians 6:9-10 (AMP)

The Waiting Process!

Patience → Endurance → Reward

Beginning → Middle → End

Do Good → Keep Doing Good → Results of Doing Good

I Forgive You

During the waiting process, the middle stage is always the most difficult part of the process because it is during this time where your feelings and your faith are in constant conflict. This is the stage where the battles are won or lost. During the mid-point in Joseph's life after receiving the vision from God, he had to be patient, continue to do what was right, and hold on to the promise (the vision God gave him). The middle stage is when you are tested most and you have to endure the temptation to respond out of your feelings when hurt and offended. Remember the three-step process to manifest forgiveness in your heart and remain committed to <u>step number one</u>: **Make the Decision to Forgive by Faith!**

Once you've made the decision to forgive, remain committed to that decision no matter what your mind and your feelings are telling you. You will know you are free from unforgiveness when the negative thoughts from your past enter into your mind and the feelings that were associated with the experiences are no long present. If you continue to struggle with unforgiveness, **<u>continue to work the three-step forgiveness process until you are totally free</u>**!

- Make the decision to forgive by faith
- Resist the temptation to act out of your emotions.
- Take control over negative thoughts by speaking positive words about your situation or offender.

The Key to Freedom

I recommend that you pray Psalm 51 in its entirety twice a day to develop the "heart attitude" necessary to walk in forgiveness.

Cleanse Me O Lord!

"Have mercy on me, O God, according to Your lovingkindness; According to the greatness of Your compassion blot out my transgressions. Wash me thoroughly from my wickedness and guilt and cleanse me from my sin. For I am conscious of my transgressions and I acknowledge them; My sin is always before me. Against You, You only, have I sinned And done that which is evil in your sight, So that You are justified when You speak (Your sentence) And faultless in Your judgment. I was brought forth in (a state of) wickedness; In sin my mother conceived me (and from my beginning I, too, was sinful). Behold, You desire truth in the innermost being, And in the hidden part (of my heart) You will make me know wisdom. Purify me with hyssop, and I will be clean; Wash me, and I will be whiter than snow. Make me to hear joy and gladness and be satisfied; Let the bones which You have broken rejoice. Hide Your face from my sins And blot out all my iniquities. <u>Create in me a clean heart, O God, And renew a right and steadfast</u>

<u>spirit within me.</u> Do not cast me away from Your presence And do not take Your Holy Spirit from me. Restore to me the joy of Your salvation And sustain me with a willing spirit. Then I will teach transgressors Your ways, And sinners shall be converted and return to You. Rescue me from blood guiltiness, O God, the God of my salvation; Then my tongue will sing joyfully of Your righteousness and Your justice. O Lord, open my lips, That my mouth may declare Your praise. For You do not delight in sacrifice, or else I would give it; You are not pleased with burnt offering. My (only) sacrifice (acceptable) to God is a broken spirit; <u>A broken and contrite heart (broken with sorrow for sin, thoroughly penitent)</u>, such, O God, You will not despise. By Your favor do good to Zion; May You rebuild the walls of Jerusalem. Then will You delight in the sacrifices of righteousness, In burnt offering and whole burnt offering; Then young bulls will be offered on Your alter."

- Psalm 51:1-19 (AMP)

"The Power of Forgiveness is The Love of God in Action"

The power of forgiveness was God's love in action when He gave His son Jesus Christ to atone for the sins of all humanity. When Jesus died on the cross, God at that point, considered every person forgiven of all sin! Jesus paid the price for sin so that we would be exempt from the penalty of death. God, who is full of mercy and love, forgave us so that we would have the hope of eternal life.

> **For God so (greatly) loved and dearly prized the world, that He (even) gave His (One and) only begotten Son so that whoever believes and trusts in Him (as Savior) shall not perish, but have eternal life. For God did not send the Son into the world to judge and condemn the world (that is, to initiate the final judgment of the world), but that the world might be saved through Him."**
>
> - John 3:16-17 (AMP)

God sent Jesus Christ into the world so that whoever believes on Him shall not perish, be rejected, be condemned, or receive the death sentence for the wages of sin. Jesus brought salvation, which means you and I can once and for all be reconciled back in right standing with God. The devil knows that if you receive the Word of God in your heart, that Word has the power to grow and deliver you from sin, bitterness, and unforgiveness. The Word has the power to compel you to love and forgive your enemies. Once you understand that you have been forgiven, satan can no longer torment you with your past.

God forgave you and I so that we could walk in total freedom! God wants you and I to forgive others so

I Forgive You

that we can manifest His peace that surpasses all understanding in our lives. After the Apostle Paul received God's forgiveness in his life, he walked away from his horrible past and claimed his new future in Christ. Paul began to focus on the prize of the upward call of God in Christ Jesus. God wants you and I to be like Paul and confess our sins, forget our past, and press towards the mark of the high calling in Christ Jesus!

> **"Brothers and sisters, I do not consider that I have made it my own yet; but one thing I do: forgetting what lies behind and reaching forward to what lies ahead, I press on toward the goal to win the (heavenly) prize of the upward call of God in Christ Jesus."**
> – Philippians 3:13-14 (AMP)

Forgiveness is the Key to Freedom!

Chapter V: Forgiveness, The Key to Freedom!

Key Principles

- Unresolved unforgiveness is self-destructive!
- When you forgive it doesn't free your accuser, forgiveness liberates you!
- Forgiveness is a gift you give yourself!
- Forgiveness releases you from your past and positions you to embrace your future!
- Forgiveness releases God's will and purpose for your life!
- Your position in life speaks to your mission in life!
- Forgiveness is a matter of the heart!
- The power of forgiveness is God's love in action!

Meditation Scriptures

Ephesians 4:32
"Be kind and helpful to one another, tender-hearted (compassionate, understanding) forgiving one another (readily and freely), just as God in Christ also forgave you."

Matthew 6:14
"For if you do not forgive others (nurturing your hurt and anger with the result that it interferes with your relationship with God), then your Father will not forgive your trespasses."

I Forgive You

John 8:36
"So if the Son makes you free, then you are unquestionably free."

1 John 1:9
"If we (freely) admit that we have sinned and confess our sins, He is faithful and just (true to His own nature and promises), and will forgive our sins and cleanse us continually from all unrighteousness (our wrongdoing, everything not in conformity with His will and purpose)."

Romans 4:7
"Blessed and happy and to be envied are those whose iniquities are forgiven and whose sins are covered up and completely buried!"

Proverbs 4:23
"Keep vigilant watch over your heart; that's where life starts."

Galatians 5:22-23
"But the fruit of the Spirit (the result of His presence within us) is love (unselfish concern for others), joy (inner) peace, patience (not the ability to wait, but how we act while waiting), kindness, goodness, faithfulness, gentleness, self-control."

Luke 21:19
"By your (patient) endurance (empowered by the Holy Spirit) you will gain your souls."

Chapter V: Reflection Questions

Why is forgiveness the key to freedom? Explain the direct correlation between forgiveness and freedom.

_____
_____
_____
_____
_____
_____
_____
_____

Reflect on a personal situation in your life when you were lied on or mistreated. Are you still struggling with forgiving the person(s)? If so, how can you incorporate the Three-Step Process to forgive, and move forward in life?

_____
_____
_____
_____
_____
_____

I Forgive You

Reflect on the waiting process of forgiveness. What part of this process is the biggest challenge for you? Is it the beginning, middle, or end? Please explain in detail.

_____
_____
_____
_____
_____
_____
_____
_____

As you reflect on the chapter and some of the personal information that the author shared about his life experiences, ask yourself the following questions:

- **What?**
- **So, what?**
- **Now, what?**

Begin with defining and sharing **"what"** facts and events the author shared in the chapter, *"Forgiveness, The Key to Freedom."*

"So, what" did you learn about yourself as a result of what the author shared?

"Now, what" learning occurred for you as a result of this shared experience? How will you apply what

The Key to Freedom

you learned to help you embrace forgiveness in your life? Use the reflection notes to respond.

Personal Reflection Notes:

I Forgive You

The Key to Freedom

Salvation

To the millions of people who are seeking love around the world, I give you an open invitation to true love. This love that I'm talking about is a love that forgives, comforts, heals, restores, delivers, protects, preserve, and prospers. This love that I'm talking about gives an unspeakable joy and a peace that surpasses all understanding. This love that I am talking about has a desire to give, and never take. The only thing that this love takes away is your sadness, sickness, poverty, pain, and spiritual death. You may be asking yourself, "what kind of love can do this?" **The love of God** is the love that will never fail you or forsake you. The love of God is the only love that can cover a multitude of sin!

"For God so greatly loved and dearly prized the world that He (even) gave up His only begotten (unique) Son, so that whoever believes in (trusts in, clings to, relies on) Him shall not perish (come to destruction, be lost) but have eternal (everlasting)

life. For God did not send the Son into the world in order to judge (to reject, to condemn, to pass sentence on) the world, but that the world might find salvation and be made safe and sound through Him."

- John 3:16-17 (AMP)

"So if the Son liberates you (makes you free men), then you are really and unquestionably free!"
- John 8:36 (AMP)

Are you ready to be free?

God has ordained purpose, greatness, and destiny for your life. You have value and worth in the eyes of God! Don't believe the lies of the enemy. Satan wants you to think that you messed up your life so bad that nothing can help you. This is a LIE! The only sin that is unforgiven, is the sin that is not confessed! It doesn't matter what you did in your past. It doesn't matter what how people treat you or view you as a person. The only thing that matters is that God loves you and Jesus paid the price for you to be forgiven and freed from your past! The question is, are you ready to be free? Are you ready to change the course of your life forever?

If your answer is yes, then, say "yes" to Jesus today!

Repeat after me:

Dear Lord, I come to you now just as I am. You know my life and You know how I've lived. I repent of my sin! I ask You to forgive me! Wash me with Your precious blood! I believe Jesus Christ is the Son of God and He died for my sin. On the third day, Jesus was raised from the dead. Lord Jesus, I ask You to come into my life, and live Your life in me and through me. Fill my heart with your love.

I renounce the devil and I receive Jesus as my new Lord and Savior today! Holy Spirit, have Your way in my life from this day forward. Thank You Lord that You have a plan for my life, and "greatness" is my destiny! Lord, keep me forgiven with You and forgiving others in Jesus Name! Amen

I want to personally congratulate you! When you except Jesus Christ into your heart, all your sins are forgiven. The Bible calls this experience the "born-again" experience. This experience is not a natural experience, but a spiritual experience! When you become "born-again," it's not an outward change, but an inward change. Your physical body remains the same. However, your spiritual nature has changed and has become one with God. You are now a new creation in Christ!

"Therefore, if anyone is in Christ (that is, grafted in, joined to Him by faith as Savior), he is a new creature (reborn and renewed by the Holy Spirit); the old things (the previous moral and spiritual condition) has passed away. Behold, new things have come (because spiritual awakening brings a new life)."
– II Corinthians 5:17 (AMP)

~ Welcome to the Family of God! ~

Forgiveness Confession
I Forgive You!
T. Dwayne Smith, Sr.

Father, I forgive as You have forgiven me. I turn from the cheek of retaliation to the cheek of love. Therefore, I forgive those who have hurt me, and who has purposed in their hearts to hate and persecute me! Forgive them Father for they know not what they do! I ask that You would deal with them according to Your loving kindness. Use me to display Your love that draws the wicked to repent.

In the Name of Jesus, I clothe myself with compassion, kindness, humility, gentleness, patience, and love. Love is patient. Love is kind. Love is not easily angered, and love keeps no record of wrong doing. Love does not delight in evil but rejoices with the truth. Love perseveres and love never fails!

Therefore, I let go and release all hurt, pain, resentment, disappointment, anger, wrath, strife, offense, divisiveness, bitterness, malice, hatred, and rage from my heart. I refuse to allow people and life circumstances to discourage me from fulfilling the will of God in my life. In the name of Jesus, I bind you satan! I rebuke you and I cast down every thought and vein imagination in Jesus's name! Thank You Lord for creating in me a clean heart and renewing in me a right spirit!

I decree that the peace of Christ reigns in my heart. Therefore, I walk in peace and in harmony with everyone that I come in contact with today. I am the righteousness of God through Christ Jesus! I am free from my past and I'm walking in God's perfect will for my life from this day forward in Jesus's name.

Amen

Prayer of Restoration for Backsliders
I Forgive You
T. Dwayne Smith, Sr.

Father, forgive me for walking away from your grace, mercy, and salvation. Lord, I confess my sin (name the sin(s) you have committed), and I thank You for cleansing me of all unrighteousness according to 1 John 1:9.

Forgive me Lord and restore me like the "Lost Son" was forgiven and restored by his father. I need Your forgiveness and restoration because I want to come home. Like David prayed in Psalms 51:10-12 (NIV): "Create in me a pure heart and renew a steadfast spirit within me. Do not cast me from your presence or take Your Holy Spirit from me. Restore to me the joy of Your salvation and grant me a willing spirit, to sustain me."

Thank You Lord for restoring my life, my health, my peace, my joy, my family, my finances, and the assignment You have for my life. I receive restoration in my life now by faith in Jesus's Name!

Now, I will teach transgressors Your ways and sinners will turn back to You as I have turned back to You. My tongue will sing of Your righteousness. My mouth will declare Your praise because You are my God and You love me!

Thank You Lord for never giving up on me, leaving me, nor forsaking me. I seal this prayer in Jesus's name!

Amen

I WANT TO HEAR FROM YOU!

Please write a book review on Amazon!

And feel free to send your written testimony tdwayne@teamunstoppable.solutions

Please be sure to check out the **companion workbook / journal** that goes along with this book: **I Forgive You, A Daily Walk of Forgiveness** available on Amazon or by request wherever books are sold.

Other Books by T. Dwayne Smith, Sr.
- **The Process Equals the Product Book**
  - **The Process Equals the Product Life Application Workbook**
- **The Process Book**
  - **The Process Life Application Workbook**